Foreword by Scot McKnight
CHRIS FOLMSBEE

STORY SIGNS AND SACRED RHYTHMS

A NARRATIVE APPROACH TO YOUTH MINISTRY

 youth specialties

ZONDERVAN.com/
AUTHORTRACKER
follow your favorite authors

ZONDERVAN

Story, Signs, and Sacred Rhythms: A Narrative Approach to Youth Ministry
Copyright © 2010 by Chris Folmsbee

YS Youth Specialties is a trademark of YOUTHWORKS!, INCORPORATED and is registered with the United States Patent and Trademark Office.

Requests for information should be addressed to:

Zondervan, *Grand Rapids, Michigan 49530*

Library of Congress Cataloging-in-Publication Data

Folmsbee, Chris.
    Story, signs, and sacred rhythms: a narrative approach to youth ministry
/ Chris Folmsbee.
        p. cm.
    Includes bibliographical references
    ISBN 978-0-310-29199-2
    1. Church group work with youth 2. Narrative theology. I. Title.
BV4447.F63 2010
259'.23—dc22   2001017679

Cover and Interior design by SharpSeven Design.

Printed in the United States of America

---

10 11 12 13 14 15 • 24 23 22 21 20 19 18 17 16 15 14 13 12 11 10 9 8 7 6 5 4 3 2 1

For Megan, Drew, and Luke

CONTENTS

8 Preface

12 Prayers

15 Acknowledgments

17 Introduction

20 Chapter 1—A Narrative Approach

32 Chapter 2—Narrative and Mission

50 **Part One: Story**

52 Chapter 3—Preparation: God's Story as the Context for Discovering God's Mission

66 Chapter 4—Revelation: God's Story as the Context for Our Participation in God's Mission

80 Chapter 5—Foundation: God's Story as the Context for Our Theology

94 **Part Two: Signs**

96 Chapter 6—Implication: God's Story as the Context for Our Identity and Calling

120 Chapter 7—Integration: God's Story as the Context for Our Way of Life

132 **Part Three: Sacred Rhythms**

134 Chapter 8—Application: God's Story as the Context for Our Behaviors and Expressions

148 Chapter 9—Implementation: Realizing a Narrative Approach to Youth Ministry

164 Epilogue

174 Appendices

180 Endnotes

FOREWORD

For a decade I either ignored or diminished the oft-made claims that the rising generations of teenagers and young adults were different. *Yada, yada, yada. Every generation has its own hype,* so I thought. Time and observation, and some reluctant listening, broke down my *yada, yada, yadas* and brought about a complete conversion in my thinking. Pastors and professors are without question facing new challenges with youth today. In fact, the challenges may well be unlike anything they've ever faced.

Some sociologists think this current generation should be labeled Generation Me, and they are not afraid to lay the blame on my generation, often called the Me Generation. This generation may well have the most robust egos in history and can show all the signs of being self-absorbed. But it would be a colossal mistake to brush this generation aside as a bundle of little narcissists. Here's why: It is also a generation loaded with the potency to fight for what is right in ways previous generations, strapped as they were to duty and loyalty, never imagined. This so-called iGeneration may well prove to be the most weGeneration in history.

This burgeoning, blossoming generation needs ministry that challenges in ways unlike the past. It needs a theology that begins in new places, and it needs a vision that outstrips what many of us grew up with.

Chris Folmsbee is a new kind of youth minister for a new kind of youth, and in this book he offers a breathtaking sketch of what youth ministry can, and I hope will, be. *Story, Signs, and Sacred Rhythms* is profoundly theological. (And I have to go on record saying youth ministry books could use a lot more theological reflection.) But don't get me wrong; this isn't some old-fashioned systematic theology ramped up for a new age or dressed in hipster clothing to bait today's youth. Instead, this book offers us a narrative theology that takes the Bible's very shape so seriously it reshapes what youth ministry looks like. I can't tell you how excited I was when I sat down with Chris over lunch at Tre Kronor, a Swedish restaurant near North Park University, and he informed me he wanted to do a theology of youth ministry rooted in story. *Here,* I thought to myself, *is someone who gets it.* Whether Chris is sketching the Story itself, talking about implications and integration, or discussing spiritual practices, this book keeps showing how Story reshapes and restores youth ministry.

One of the most encouraging developments among youth ministers today is the selection and scope of their reading. I find youth ministers today, and Chris represents the trend, refreshingly in touch with Bible, theology, Church history, sociology, psychology, cultural trends, and technology. Chris' reading is wide and reflective and critical, and he has been reading the leading lights of our day. Be ready for an assortment of creative ideas.

Praxis has long been the focus of much of our thinking about youth ministry. Instead of asking probing philosophical and theological questions, too often we have been satisfied with "Okay, okay, but tell me what we should do." Not in this book. While Chris runs narrative theology through all of his thinking, and while this book does dabble in praxis and wisdom and advice, everyone who reads this book carefully will be led to ask questions. And if leaders will take the time to ponder what is in the pages of this book and have their ministry impacted by it, Generation Me will put the Me Generation to shame in what they offer the world as people who live out the kingdom vision of Jesus and participate in the mission of God in this world.

Scot McKnight
Karl A. Olsson Professor in Religious Studies
North Park University, Chicago, Illinois

Glocal =
Think globally
and act locally!

PREFACE

The Hope That Lives Within Me

I couldn't have more hope for the future of youth ministry in North America and around the world than I do right now. It's providing my heart, mind, and soul with fresh feelings, new thinking, and a new sense of direction.

I'm completely enthralled by the present trends of youth ministry, including the innovative ideas and practices, unique and artistic leadership styles of emerging leaders, creative resources and tools, diversity of the people being called to such an endeavor, and mold-shattering collaborative efforts of glocal churches.[1] I'm captivated by the church's increasing levels of passion and commitment to recognize youth as not only *valuable* players in the mission of God, but *vital* ones as well.

As I travel throughout North America to speak, train, and consult, I continually run into people who have a strong sense that if this world is going to change, as we all long for it to do, then we must begin to believe in and rely upon the rising generations. We can no longer deceive ourselves into believing that *we* (just you and me, that is) have what it takes to change the world. However, we must believe that *we* (you, me, *and* the rising generations) have what it takes to arrive and live within that desirable change.

There is a sentiment out there that, for a long time, youth ministry has just involved the task of entertaining teens. Many churches offer programs for youth with the right intentions in mind—evangelism, discipleship, missions, etc. But too often their intentions have given way to the acceptance of a lesser substitute that merely involves keeping youth busy, providing a place for them to make friends, and sending them the message, "When you're you are all grown up, we'd love to have you back as a member." You and I know this is a gross reduction of what we do, and really what has been happening in churches all over North America. Among youth workers, however, there is still a sense of a great need to refocus our efforts (and the perceptions projected on us) away from a mere entertainment approach and move toward a narrative approach that equips the rising generations for something different from anything we've ever experienced.

Presently I work with an organization in Kansas City called Youthfront. It's been around for a little more than 65 years. At Youthfront we have a passion to assist the church as it seeks to lean into and live out the mission of God. One of the ways we do this is by serving thousands of students every summer through our resident camps. The students we serve and work alongside believe in their own generation. They believe they can change the world. They trust each other and carry a very positive and poised sense that their generation not only *can* change the world, but *will* change the world. They long to end poverty, prevent war, overturn injustices, balance budgets, get rid of debt, protect and preserve the environment, eliminate racism, purge crime, and grow into a culture of what is right, just, and good—just as God created this world to be.[2] I believe in the rising generations because I believe they live by a credo that if you want to see the world change, you have to be the change you want to see.

I sincerely believe that some years down the road—when I'm much slower on this keyboard and much further removed from the word *youthful*—this world will be transformed from what we currently know and experience.

The ideals and actions I see displayed in the rising generations are energizing and inspiring. However, much of what makes me confident in the rising generations has to do with you. I believe in *you*! I believe the efforts of youth workers who've battled to get where they are today, regardless of how they assess the condition of youth ministry, have brought us into a place of unlimited possibilities. The opportunities before us are immense. We have virtually all that's necessary to equip youth to be the change we all crave, and I wholeheartedly believe youth workers will make the most of it in the coming days.

Youth workers are creative, passionate, and relentless in their quests; I thoroughly believe those traits will cause us to succeed in our work to inspire future generations to find and follow Jesus. Couple those three characteristics with a youth culture comprised of growing activists whom I believe are ready, willing, and able to make change, and you have a blueprint for a whole new world—especially when it's in pursuit of, and participation in, the mission of God.

Youth workers are an integral force to take that blueprint from a good idea or dream to a practical reality. Please don't think for one minute that the hours you spend every week giving your life away to the youth and their families in your church and community are in vain. Every little thing and every big thing you do is an essential ingredient to the establishment of a whole new world. Actually, as my friend Mark reminds me from time to time, there are no little things, just specific things. Every specific thing you do deeply matters.

Youth culture, the youth worker community, and the church are all positioned and pleading for change. I'm equally as hopeful that the church is ready, willing, and able to become what it needs to be and what it's called to be to make way for a whole new world to emerge. As we'll discuss more intensively as this book proceeds, the church, both local and global, is the body of Christ—a gathering of divergent people who believe God reigns over all and Jesus is Lord and Savior. The church is a people—a people who find authentic community with one another knowing who they are, what they're to be about, and why they're to be about it. Simply put, the church is a community of missionary people who are the visible signs of Christ revealing the missionary heart of God.

In the words of Teresa of Avila—

> Christ has no body now on earth but yours;
>
> Yours are the only hands with which He can do His work.
>
> Yours are the only feet with which He can go about the world;
>
> Yours are the only eyes through which His compassion can shine forth upon a troubled world.
>
> Christ has no body on earth but yours.[3]

I believe the church is going to make the most of the recent confusion and unrest. I contend that the recent conversations in North America (everything from the emergent church to the new perspective on Paul to the conversations surrounding homosexuality) have been good for the church. Regardless of which camp you reside in, you have to admit that these conversations have stimulated thinking, created much needed dialogue, encouraged honesty, sparked the imagination, defined purpose, set direction, called for commitment, reclaimed theology over methodology, and pushed people to learn new insights.

It's also true that recent conversations have been divisive at times. Even still, one who loves the mission of the church must—at the very least—be thankful for what the conversations have done to infuse passion, grow character, and sharpen convictions—making a community of people who think and live in harmony. I believe these conversations, as difficult as they've been, have called us all to something bigger than any one particular person or group of people and their ideas or practices. I truly believe the unrest we've experienced over the last decade or so has helped us to fall in love with the church more deeply. For that reason, I'm hopeful that as the church continues in its forever reforming ways, we'll seek to be the blueprint for and the establishment of a whole new world. I pray the church stands ready, willing, and able to come together to seek change, see change, and be the change we all eagerly want.

PRAYERS

A PRAYER FOR TODAY'S CHURCH

A few years ago, when I was transitioning from a youth pastor position in a church in Burnsville, Minnesota, to the president of Sonlife near Chicago, Illinois, one of my mentors and spiritual directors, named Mark Patrick, gave me a book by Arthur A. Rouner Jr. called *Someone's Praying, Lord.* Below is an excerpt from a prayer that Mark chose from the book—one that he wanted me to remember as I embarked on a new role from ministering *in* the church to ministering *to* the church.

Dear God, this is Your Church.

We don't own it. You own us.

You called us to live Your life, to do Your work,

to see Your vision and dream Your dream.

If what we've talked about today is not Your will,

if it's not Divine but of the Devil—destroy it, Lord,

before we take one step.

Show us by some sign that it is wrong, all wrong!

But if it's right—God, help us move!

Help us move out and claim that future,

help us take our stand, and be the church

You put us here to be.

Oh, Jesus Christ,

who gave Your life away to show Your Church how it might live:

Don't let us be afraid of the adventure.

Don't let us pale at the thought of giving away

more than we ever had before.

And don't let us have faint hearts when we are faced with

the chance to do something big,

something dangerous, something difficult.[4]

A PRAYER FOR TODAY'S YOUTH

Below is a prayer I often pray for today's youth. It comes from the heart of Frederick Buechner, a man I've always admired and sought to learn from. I want to encourage you to take a moment to pray this prayer for today's youth right now. Perhaps this prayer, or others like it, might become a part of your daily rhythms.

Be present especially with the young who must choose between many voices. Help them to know how much an old world needs their youth and gladness. Help them to know that there are words of truth and healing that will never be spoken unless they speak them, and deeds of compassion and courage that will never be done unless they do them. Help them never to mistake success for victory or failure for defeat. Grant that they may never be entirely content with whatever bounty the world may bestow upon them, but that they may know at last that they were created not for happiness but for joy, and that joy is to him alone who, sometimes with tears in his eyes, commits himself in love to thee and his brothers. Lead them and all thy world ever deeper into the knowledge that finally all men are one and that there can never really be joy for any until there is joy for all. In Christ's name we ask it and for his sake. Amen.[5]

A PRAYER FOR TODAY'S YOUTH WORKER

I came across this prayer by Walter Rauschenbusch, from his book *For God and the People*, some time ago when I was preparing to address a number of youth ministers and teachers at a conference near Cleveland, Ohio. I read it often as I try to continually reframe my role as an educator of the things of God.

We implore thy blessing, O God, on all the men and women who teach the children and youth of our nation, for they are the potent friends and helpers of our homes. Into their hands we daily commit the dearest that we have, as they make our children, so shall future years see them. Grant them an abiding consciousness that they are co-workers with thee, thou great teacher of humanity, and that thou hast charged them with the holy duty of bringing forth from the budding life of the young the mysterious stores of character and the ability which thou has hidden in them. Teach them to reverence the young lives, clean and plastic, which have newly come from thee, and to realize that generations still unborn shall rue their sloth or rise to higher levels through their wisdom and faithfulness. Gird them for their task with thy patience and tranquility, with a great fatherly and motherly love for the young, and with special tenderness for the backward and afflicted. Save them from physical exhaustion, from loneliness and discouragement, from the numbness of routine, and from all bitterness of the heart.[6]

ACKNOWLEDGMENTS

Thanks to the hundreds of you who helped shape this book through our conversations, prayers, dreams, and experiments.

Thanks to Matt Wilks, Doug Jones, Michael Novelli, and Seth McCoy for their creative input and editorial contributions over the last couple of years.

Thanks to Jamie Roach, Mike King, and Erik Leafblad for helping me most effectively structure the ideas in the book. Thanks also to Kurt Rietema, Melanie Hill, Tim Ciccone, Nate Severson, Dustin Angell, Craig Lueck, Rick Rhodes, Nathan Vawser, Dana Nearmyer, Aaron Mitchum, and Dennis and Kyle Palombo for their feedback and input.

Thanks to Jay Howver for giving me yet another shot at publishing my ideas.

Thanks to Scot McKnight for writing the Foreword, his distant mentorship, and his many works that contributed to this project.

Thanks to all of the staff at Youthfront, especially Topher Philgreen, Jim Newberry, and Dustin Angell, who have given of themselves to go beyond the ordinary in order that this book might be written.

Thanks to my friends at Youth Specialties who allowed me the privilege of engaging people in conversation regarding the matters in this book at their National Youth Workers Conventions. A special thanks to Marko and Tic for their friendship and support.

Thanks to the many people at Church of the Resurrection, my family's faith community, who model a commitment to the missio Dei, and especially to Pastor Adam Hamilton, who provides leadership and inspiration to us all, and Jason Gant, who does a fantastic job leading our youth ministry.

Thanks to Mark and Polly Patrick for their friendship and for passing on their wisdom for life and ministry to my wife and me.

Thanks to Frank Mercadante for the many wonderful conversations that helped shape much of the thinking in this book.

Thanks to Matt and Doug. Your ongoing friendships mean the world to me.

Thanks to my wife, Gina, of course. Thanks for sacrificing so much while I locked myself in a room to write this book. And thanks for your love, friendship, and encouragement.

INTRODUCTION

A couple of years ago, I published my first book, entitled *A New Kind of Youth Ministry*. The book did exactly what my publisher, Jay Howver, and I hoped it would—it got youth workers thinking deeper and talking further. The book started (or continued) conversations concerning current youth ministry methods and various perspectives on aspects of youth ministry such as evangelism, discipleship, leadership, and education. The book also guided thinking around whether or not what we're doing in youth ministry is really all that effective. Many youth workers have discerned through those conversations, of which my book was just a small part, that youth ministry needs fresh imagination, vision, strategy, and a new implementation plan in order to more deeply engage the mission of God (missio Dei).

I never intended for *A New Kind of Youth Ministry* to be a model or a design for youth ministry. I simply intended to get youth workers thinking and talking about the best and most effective ways to create and sustain environments that guide and direct students into Christian formation. I was hoping *A New Kind of Youth Ministry* would set up the book you now hold in your hands. In other words, I hoped that after reading *A New Kind of Youth Ministry*, you'd long for another book to provide you with a model you'd feel comfortable executing—one that affirms your gifts, beliefs, and efforts.

Story, Signs, and Sacred Rhythms is intended to be a model for youth ministry. It's intended to provide paid and unpaid church- and parachurch-based youth workers and volunteers around the world with an approach to youth ministry that's solidly biblical, profoundly logical, inspiringly fresh, and conclusively practical.

Like you, I want the church—and namely youth ministry—to be relevant. Nearly every day I wake up thinking about how the church can have more of a significant bearing on the spiritual development and transformation of students. This book, therefore, is intended to give you a model for ministry that's appropriately relevant to the missional church *and* the changing culture.

I'm not concerned about what's hip or trendy. Nor am I concerned about what this book does for me as an influencer in youth ministry. I'm not concerned about being right or being viewed as the guy with all the answers.

I am concerned, however, that this book will help you do better what you love doing and what you already do best—which is loving students into deeper levels of union with God.

DESIRED OUTCOMES FOR *STORY, SIGNS, AND SACRED RHYTHMS*

As any author should and most likely would, I have a few goals or desired outcomes for this book. Each of these goals is eagerly anticipated to competently and fruitfully serve you as you strive to best serve the students and families within your faith community and your local community. My goals are simply to—

- Provide you with a clear and compelling vision for a narrative-missional youth ministry.

- Provide you with a theologically rich and accurate summary of God's Story and mission.

- Inspire and challenge each of you with a community model for ministry that may even become a personal design for your own life.

- Equip you with an approach to youth ministry that enables you to create, sustain, and refine environments for Christian formation.

- Present you and your peers with a common language that encourages collaboration and shared ministry experiences.

- Provide you with a customizable model that encourages you to use your imagination and is unique to your gifts and personal composition.

- Guide you toward other authors and their various works in order that they might help as you move toward a new approach.

- Push you to assess the realities of your current ministry model or lack thereof.

- Affirm your current work while enhancing your effectiveness by giving you a ministry design that is measurable and evaluative, allowing you to refine and change course as needed.

- Transform (through you and your commitment) an emerging generation that results in many thousands of teens around the world giving their lives to join God in his mission to restore the world!

Nothing would excite me (and my wife, as she's the one who truly sacrifices as I write books) more than to know that these goals have been met when you close the back cover after finishing this book.

The mission of God is an adventure, no doubt. As we move through this book to better align our youth ministries to the missionary heart of God, we'll need to realize the big, dangerous, and difficult, yet exciting and rewarding task we have before us. I pray that we all might give way to the heart of God as we lean into and live out the mission of God.

CHAPTER 1
A Narrative Approach

Of all the acceptable prefixes available to us, I have a favorite. You read that correctly. I'm talking about those small groupings of letters we attach to the beginning of a root word in order to modify the meaning. And my favorite prefix is "re." Absolutely captivated, aren't you?

The prefix re- is my favorite simply because of its significance throughout the entire Story of God. Think about it for a moment. What are some of the most significant "re" words we find in the Bible? A small sampling would include words such as *re*demption, *re*union, *re*birth, *re*turn, *re*conciliation, *re*surrection, *re*storation, and *re*pentance. These words are all very important to understanding the overarching Story of God, as well as the various storylines, throughout the Bible as they call us to a new action.

As readers of Christian thought, over the last few years we've been challenged to *reimagine* spiritual formation, *reculture* youth ministry, *reclaim* Paul, *return* to ancient practices, and *rethink* the methods of the church. All of these words are aptly used to help us go back to the beginning or experience something again or even act (proactively or reactively) in opposition to something.

You'll find the prefix re- used throughout this book—mostly with the word *restoration*. I believe it's the mission of God to bring restoration to the world, and it's my premise that it's through our discovery and understanding of God's Story throughout history that we can first join his mission. It's my hope that those of us who work with and serve adolescents and their families under the umbrella of "youth ministry" might be compelled to move our efforts, be they in the church or community, into closer alignment with the mission of God (missio Dei) as we come to understand that mission through the entire narrative of God.

I'm attempting to do three things in this book. First, I hope to help you discover or more fully understand God's past, present, and future restorative plan and activity in the world as seen in his complete story from Genesis to Revelation.

Second, I hope you'll be inspired and compelled to realign your youth ministry efforts with God's mission to restore the world or—as I'll continually refer to it throughout this book—God's mission to restore the world to its intended wholeness. The purpose of this realignment is that we—as a community of youth workers and as a segment of the body of Christ—might be more missional in our vision, strategy, desired outcomes, and accomplishments.

Third, I hope you'll restore or reconnect with the passion and calling that's led you to pick up a copy of this book. My wish is that you might return to that wild rejection of the things of this world; return to the feelings, desires, dreams, and passions that made you take the leap from all things comfortable—that same leap that first brought you into the middle of this messy, chaotic, demanding, yet stirring work called youth ministry.

The Bible is full of stories of restoration. Jacob and Esau were restored to one another; Joseph was restored to his once hateful brothers; Job's wealth was restored to him after much suffering and pain; the Prodigal Son was restored to his father; Jesus and Peter's relationship was restored; and those of us who share a trust and faith in the claims of Jesus will one day be completely restored. God is in the process of restoring the world to its intended wholeness—all that was good, right, and just; all that was whole, and all that will become whole as God makes all things new.

THE NEED FOR NEW

A few years ago, I began experimenting with a fresh approach to youth ministry. With the help of my coworkers at the time (Michael Novelli, Matt Wilks, Doug Jones, and Seth McCoy), I began thinking more broadly about the construct I was using to help youth workers help students find and follow Jesus or lean into and live out the Story of God.[7] The model, which I call a narrative approach, was born out of dozens of hours of conversation, experimentation in local church-based youth ministries, intermittent brainstorming sessions, ongoing development of training journals, as well as hosting various learning experiences throughout North America and in other parts of the globe. Thus, the narrative model was born out of several conclusions:

1. Youth ministry needed a fresh approach.

Youth workers needed to feel the freedom to scrap what they were doing in order to find newer, more helpful methods and practices. The postmodernization of youth ministry—as a result of a consistently changing culture, coupled with what was, at the time, a fairly new development in church (think emergent conversation)—left the youth workers I encountered longing for a common, wider, yet very descriptive model of youth ministry.

Some youth workers were clamoring for a ministry model that would allow them to explore the expansive outline of the mission of God, while focusing their attention on a more detailed, missional-minded model found within the message, mission, and means of Jesus.

I found other youth workers who were simply standing fast to what they always knew in their philosophy and methodology. Common discussions on recurring themes such as biblical authority and inerrancy, defining truth, theories of atonement, and modes of salvation often became heated as youth workers (who are intensely passionate people anyway) indicated newfound measures of uncertainty, confusion, and, therefore, angst with the model I was presenting (but with any new model, really).

Largely, these uncertain and apprehensive youth workers weren't addressing theological concerns with the narrative approach that I was developing. In many ways they were revealing their aggravation with the uncertain times and the ongoing frustration of having no answers to contest the changing culture. I later realized that most of their frustrations surrounding our conversations was a symptom of a greater source of contention.

Youth workers were aware that we all needed something fresh and new, as many of us sat watching our ministries shrink, our students lose interest, and our moments of impact become more rare. (I'm generalizing here, of course.) So, I believe that much of their angst had less to do with the theology and more to do with the practical implementation of a new model (albeit theological) in what felt like a whole new world. There were some theological concerns with the narrative approach I was presenting, no doubt. However, the majority of the concerns were more about an inability to measure results in a postmodern construct than they were about the theological implications of a shift between models.

Let me clarify again that the narrative model I present here is not an attempt to find the mission of God in an approach. The mission of God remains unchanged—the restoration of the world. But this approach *does* address what we recognized as a growing need for a new way to teach youth about our involvement in the mission of God.

2. Youth workers were no longer looking for what they could plug and play.

They realized that plug-and-play might work with a gaming system and a large-screen LCD TV. But when it came to youth work, it wasn't as easy as plugging in a cable and pushing the power button. Unlike the days of going to a conference and discovering the model of ministry that was "the next best thing," youth workers were finding themselves without an appealing model of ministry. They were looking for something that fit their particular context (think localization), but most were developed too far outside of that context to genuinely give them help. Formulaic models or approaches were a dime a dozen, but none of them were scratching where most youth ministries were itching.

Because of the uniqueness of their ministry contexts, youth workers weren't looking for a *prescriptive* model. They were looking for a *descriptive* model. A descriptive model gives an expressive and vivid illustration; it provides the scaffolding or framework; and it leaves room for one's imagination, vision, risk, consideration, and care to fill it out and make it work. Descriptive models are flexible and collaborative. They require figuring it out along the way. Just as education is best aligned with experience, so a descriptive model is best aligned with experimentation.

3. Youth workers were becoming tired of the isolated deconstruction.

Nearly every book, every seminar, and every blog post on youth ministry was about what was *wrong* or *broken*. It left youth workers wanting for what might be *right* or *effective*. Youth workers are very smart people. They recognize and appreciate the need to deconstruct or to break down and dismantle the ongoing efforts of youth ministry in order to analyze what works and what doesn't. However, at some point deconstructing the current and the past has to give way to constructing something new. Today, youth workers are searching for a model of ministry that's constructing a way forward, not merely deconstructing what was. I hope the model in this book may, at least, be *one* of the ways forward.

4. Youth workers saw the need to help students learn through discovery.

It seems that for many of us, and for way too long, youth ministry was more about the volume of information we taught rather than the validation of the information from practice.

For decades many of the youth workers with whom I explored new ideas had, at some point, come to the realization that it really isn't about how much we talk about the things of God or even how *well* we talk about the things of God. Rather, the important thing is that we guide our students in imaginative exercises that help them learn about God in self-discovery kinds of ways, as opposed to others-induced kinds of ways. Many of us have come to the realization that if a student or a group of students doesn't have the foundational platform on which to develop further ideas and concepts about God once they're no longer participating in our ministries, then we've done a very poor job of preparing them for a future life of spiritual growth and discovery.

Recently, I bought my five-year-old son a toy he'd wanted for many months. When he finally received the toy, he immediately grabbed hold of it and played hard. He recklessly ran around the room while making all of the sounds he'd seen on the commercial. He moved the action figure's arms and legs in every direction possible and then launched the figure into the air as high as he could, making sure the toy landed unharmed on the couch. This lasted for all of about 10 minutes, at which point the toy's packaging became more appealing than the toy. He'd quickly realized the limitations of the toy and become bored with it. However, the box's *unlimited* possibilities made it the greater of the two.

I fear we've done this same thing with our students. We've given them a limited God. We've tried hard to present a God who isn't there for just a few minutes of their lives. But in reality, for many students God has become the toy that's eagerly awaited and then infrequently contacted. We've given them nothing more than a temporary connection to God. The narrative approach I'm presenting in this book aims at widening the lens of youth ministry, helping our students see a God who's unlimited in mission, and providing opportunities for them to join God in his activity.

5. Youth workers realized the importance of their ministry's unique context.

Context is everything, and our individual ministry contexts are, at times, overwhelmingly divergent. Regardless of your geographical location and its ethnographical composition, the locale in which you help students find and follow Jesus is distinctly different from anyone else's. There might be a church or a number of churches within several blocks of yours, but they all have a different context. Divergent contexts call for a model of ministry that isn't based on matters that are inconsistent with your context, but rather on matters that are related to the narrative and mission of God. I contend that you don't develop a ministry model and then look for how it fits into God's narrative and mission. On the contrary, we begin with a wide lens looking at the narrative and mission of God, and then we seek to find specific ways in which to embody our local contexts within the narrative and mission of God.

6. Youth workers were looking for a solid model with flexibility.

Youth workers wanted features and benefits from a model of ministry that was divergent to the core purpose. In other words, youth workers wanted a model that was unapologetically clear and compelling, but at the same time would allow for the unexpected or the unpredictable.

Being imaginative in nature, youth workers want a model of ministry that allows for the complexity, mystery, and the awe of God to come forth in places and in manifestations they never dreamed possible or plausible. Youth workers are bored with the conventional model that, due to its narrow margin of innovation and imagination, is merely a canned and methodical experience. True, youth ministry isn't solely about the feelings and fortunes of the youth worker. Nonetheless, without innovative and imaginative opportunity, youth workers look for new places and ways (outside of youth ministry) to do ministry in an environment where there's a greater likelihood of the unpredictable becoming a frequent occurrence.

7. Youth workers look for the hidden side of everything.

Youth workers are not only diligently looking at how they can influence the setting in which they presently find themselves, but they're also looking for a *wiki*-type environment where they can collaborate in and contribute to a joint venture—a co-mission, if you will, that's bigger than they are. All types of youth workers are longing for the ability to find the hidden gems within a particular model or approach. They aren't looking for an approach to youth ministry that's complete and finished. Instead, they're looking for a model that's in process, incomplete, and, therefore, in a position to be influenced by the youth workers' thinking, strategy, and implementation ideas.

The narrative approach of youth ministry allows for and is receptive to unique contributions, personal preferences, and creative thought. Models of ministry that don't take a full-orbed entire narrative perspective are models that are simply doing an injustice to God's mission and objective to restore the world to its intended wholeness. You can't take a series of cool-sounding verses from the book of Micah, one verse from the gospels, a passage from Paul's epistles, or even the Great Commission and build an entire model for ministry. An effective ministry model begins at the beginning and ends, well, at the beginning—God's mission.

A NARRATIVE APPROACH

You'll find a lot of theology throughout the rest of this book. Not long ago I was facilitating a training experience at a convention, when a gentleman (who I'm sure meant well) said, "This is good stuff, but it seems to be more about theology than youth ministry."

Youth ministry is a theological endeavor. There is absolutely no escaping that reality. You can't do youth ministry without it being deeply theological. Well, I take that back. I guess you *could* do youth ministry outside of theology, and, unfortunately, people do. However, a youth ministry rooted in nothing more than social constructs cannot hope to accomplish the mission of God. In other words theology, or the language we use to give terms for and meaning to God and the actions we live out accordingly, is the reason we have a segment in the church called "youth ministry." A youth ministry without theology is like playing basketball without a ball, fishing without line, or trying to watch music instead of listening to it. The motions might be fun to perform—they might even keep you busy—but they aren't an origin for anything. Youth ministry, in any form, without an overriding and guiding theological umbrella is hollow and inconsequential.

My approach, which I believe is worth experimenting with in your own youth ministry, is built around three main areas of relatedness: (1) Story, (2)

Signs, and (3) Sacred Rhythms. As we go through this book, we'll be looking at aspects of a narrative approach that's distinctly about God's Story (the Bible) and the signs of God, which are God's images and metaphors to guide our living.

Furthermore, this book is also about the saintly cadences that provide the connection between God and mission, as understood through God's entire narrative and as realized through a changing culture of teenagers. This book isn't describing a new program or suggesting a set of innovative activities for you to put into practice in your youth ministry. Instead, it is the concepts and ideologies of what could be for you a new way of thinking about and doing youth ministry.

On the next page you'll see an illustration that we'll use throughout this book to help guide us as we discover a new way to look at the Christian formation of the students we serve. Before I explain the illustration, it's important to note a few things.

First, please know that others share this illustration, and the language used within it is meant purely to be a starting point for you.[8] My hope is that you'll view it as a guide to help you contextualize your own illustration to use in your own setting. When I train people in the ideas found in the illustration below, I have a common phrase that goes like this: "Right click. Synonym select." In other words, choose the word that best describes what you hope to accomplish and use it.

Second, the illustration is flat—as you might expect it to be on the page of a book. Nonetheless, when they're lived out, the concepts of this illustration are hardly flat. In fact, I think you might find that the dynamic elements of this approach give you the freedom to enter into it on a variety of levels. As you make your way through this approach, look for ways to make this flat illustration more dynamic or robust. Again, this illustration and the ideas that comprise it are free for you to take and do with as you wish. This book is meant to be a starting point. Remember, we live in a *wiki* world! So take ownership of these ideas and make them fit into your unique context.

Finally, and perhaps most importantly, this book and the illustration on the next page are designed to help you evaluate your current youth ministry. Sometimes our efforts aren't that far off—they just need a little assessment and tweaking to become more effective. This might be the case for many of you. After all, this model came out of my conversations with hundreds of youth workers. And beyond that, I realize you're bright people who are well on your way.

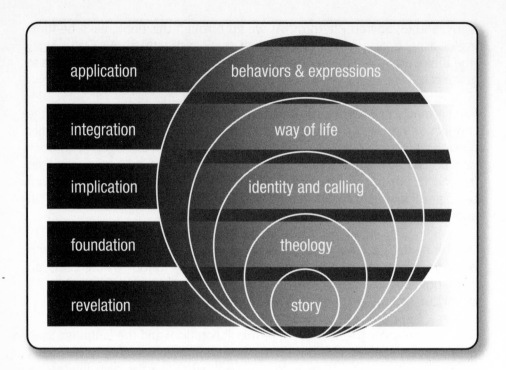

NARRATIVE FORMATION

The Story of God informs the entire structure for this model. The Story of God and its ensuing mission provides us with a comprehensive and expandable approach for youth ministry, for it's out of the Story of God that we more fully understand (Revelation) who God is, what God is like, our relationship to God, and what God is doing in the world around us. Revelation, or the way God makes himself known to us, is the starting point. I contend here—and will again throughout this book—that it's only out of God revealing his heart to us that we can begin to construct an approach to youth ministry.

The Story of God informs our theology (Foundation). The language we use to describe God and the associated actions we live out provide ongoing evidence to the world around us that God is who *he* says he is and God is who *we* say he is.

The foundation that's built for us throughout God's Story enables us to take theology from merely an intellectual assent to a practical reality. It's out of our theology that we ultimately end up living the way we do. It's in this foundation that we begin to be guided by matters of the faith, such as the kingdom, the gospel, salvation, and many others. It's my contention that the Foundation that's built within us—and that we continue to build upon—can best be informed by the Revelation of God or God's Story.

Our theology informs our identity and calling (Implication). It's out of our theological convictions that we're able to identify with questions such as *Who am I? Whose am I? Why am I here? What am I to be about in life? How does my life fit in with Jesus' life?* It's at this stage in the model that we help our students become aware of the general and specific calling in their lives and find meaning in their images and in their stories. It's also at this stage that we help our students determine how they're connected to and involved in God's enduring and unfolding drama.

The identification with our identity and calling informs our way of life (Integration). The Integration stage involves helping students synthesize all that they've experienced and come to know about God's Story, their theological foundation, and how they're involved in God's mission to develop a set of values or virtues they'll use to continue to shape their lives.

It's at this stage that students begin developing a description of Jesus against which they can measure their lives. It's at this stage that Christian formation is healthily reduced down to the Jesus creed, which is to love God and love others.[9] It's here that students recognize the importance of a faithful Jesus-centered life that isn't left void of context and meaning. Rather, it's a Jesus-centered life that's discovered not merely out of the four Gospels but out of the entire narrative of God. This discovery grounds students in their identities and calling, their theology, and their understanding of God's mission, which most illustratively comes from the merger of God's narrative and the physical presence of Jesus (as lived out by Christians who enter into the lives of others).

Our way of life informs our behaviors and expressions (Application). And our informed behaviors and expressions drive the way we interact with people, the priorities we seek to live out, and the things we do every day to cooperate with God's mission to restore the world to its intended wholeness.

Our behaviors and expressions lead us to a kingdom way of life—a missional lifestyle that originates out of God's mission and ultimately finds itself among God's handiwork: His people. It's at this stage that our students truly walk as Jesus walked and proclaim and perform the gospel. Without a way

of life, the recognition of their identity and calling, a theological foundation, and an understanding of who God is based on how God has revealed
himself to us through his Story, our students are left to discern a life of faith
on their own without context and meaning. This leaves a generation of
students who are being called to live like Jesus wanting to know why and
how. Frankly, if our students don't understand why and how, then we really
haven't helped them.

We're going to take the rest of this book to look at each of the stages of
narrative youth ministry mentioned above. I intend to show you a way forward—out of unnecessary confusion and unwanted commotion and into a
ministry model comprised of reality and formation.

revelation	foundation	implication	integration	application
how we begin to understand and know God	faith moves from an intellectual pursuit and exercise to a practical reality	we become aware of the general and specific calling on our lives and find meaning in our images and stories	synthesizing all that we have come to know and experience to develop a set of values or virtues that continue to shape our lives	the way we interact with people, the priorities we seek to live out, and the things we do every day to cooperate with God's mission

Reflection and Discussion Questions
Chapter 1—A Narrative Approach

• What are some of your current frustrations with youth ministry?
  Doesn't really prepare students for a spiritual life.

• What encourages you about the current state of youth ministry?
  It sensing that it needs to change.

• Which concerns you more: New methods of youth ministry practices really working or the theological frameworks in which they're put forth? Explain. *Theological framework. If it is based in good theology then it is useless.*

• In what ways do you see yourself advancing a limited view of God to your students?

• In what ways are you helping your students with an unlimited view of God? *Teaching open-mindedly and letting them discover God in a variety of ways.*

• What are the uniquenesses of your ministry and cultural context?

• Do you agree with the statement: "Youth ministry is a theological endeavor"? Why or why not?

• On a scale of 1 to 10, with 10 being the best, how do you feel your current philosophy and model of youth ministry are working?

• In what ways are you currently helping your students develop context and meaning for God's mission? How might you do a better job?

CHAPTER 2
Narrative and Mission

Not by any stretch of the imagination am I a theologian in the classic understanding of the word. I'm not one of the few who's been called to spend my life engaging with other scholars at intellectual levels that are usually reserved for academia. I don't regularly sit around with scholarly types and contemplate ideas about God, as do many of my friends. I enjoy having deep theological conversations and reading theologically rich books. And I certainly love bantering around the things of God on blogs. But a theologian I am not.

Like many of you, however, I'm a theologian only in the sense that I'm a student of God—albeit a novice, however, not an expert. I'm a learner of God who's trying to live out the theology that I've come to discover and comprehend. I must (we must) be a theologian in that sense if I'm going to authentically join God in his restorative activity throughout the world.

I know enough about theology to know there are many classifications, such as narrative theology, biblical theology, systematic theology, historical theology, creation theology, integrative theology, liberation theology, and so on. I, like many of you, was schooled in what's commonly referred to as systematic theology.

Systematic theology organizes and categorizes information—or what we come to learn about God—into divisions or areas. These divisions are intended to help Christians understand the fundamental doctrines of our faith more easily. For example, systematic theology would take all of the information about salvation that's found throughout the entire Bible and clump it together into one category called *soteriology*—the doctrine of salvation. The same would be true for the study of God as Father (Paterology), the study of Jesus (Christology), the study of the Holy Sprit (Pneumatology), and so on.

But for the purposes of this book, I want to look at a very different way of organizing ideas about God—narrative theology.

NARRATIVE THEOLOGY DEFINED

In what's probably its simplest definition, *narrative theology* is conversation about God in the setting of a story. We know this story as the Bible. Narrative theology in its three integrative aspects of biblical text, faith communities, and cultural contexts is perhaps the broadest way in which to understand God. It's "an account of characters and events in a plot moving over time and space through conflict toward resolution."[10]

Narrative theology is primarily about exactly what you might assume: Story and doctrine. However, narrative theology is more than a mere story. Without the accompanying doctrine that "intends to point to and signify the reality of God," the narrative of God would have no more authority nor hold any more truth than some of the greatest stories ever written.[11] And the doctrine within the Story is more than just a collection of propositions as well. As Charles Van Engen so clearly states in *Mission on the Way*, narrative theology is "broader and deeper than dogmatic propositions."[12] Van Engen gives us four reasons why narrative theology is more than propositions.

First, narrative theology accounts for a community of faith. This means that the narrative of God is also a story about people. Clearly the people of Israel and the early church are major indicators of who God is throughout the entire narrative. One can suppose, therefore, that God wishes to reveal not only himself to generations coming and going, but also what it means for humanity to work together to live in the intended ways of God.

Second, Van Engen offers this: God places himself in the midst of human history. Theology isn't meant to be a distant set of theories and speculations. Rather, theology is very much about how God interacts with people to form human history. Narrative theology is not only about a community of God's people, but also about how God and his people interrelate. From the beginning of the Story, we see God's passion for relationship and intimacy with his creation. Therefore, we might conclude that narrative theology is bigger than a set of propositions, as propositions are often so closed.

Third, narrative theology is about being on a "faith pilgrimage." God's revelation is as much about the spirituality of a wandering people as it is about God's propositions. God chooses to reveal the journey he shared with the people of Israel and the church to call others to be pilgrim people—people on the move who are traveling as God leads them, not as they desire to go. Far too often in our youth ministries, we neglect the concept of pilgrimage. We talk incessantly about faith being a journey—and rightfully so. But seldom do we connect the journey of faith with God's direction of us—as both individuals and as a community of travelers.

And for me, the word *journey* doesn't encapsulate the holy wandering of a holy people quite like the word *pilgrimage* does. A journey is a trip, expedition, voyage, passage, and so on. A pilgrimage is also a trip, but it's a trip leading to a special place—a place of wholeness and restoration. Narrative theology calls God's people to a life of pilgrimage—a life of holy wandering in which the mystical and mysterious hold as much worth as stability and security. We're all on a pilgrimage into the unknown, and the only way to survive is to trust God.

Finally, Van Engen suggests that narrative theology integrates God's words and actions. Furthermore, it allows for the actions of God to give context, meaning, and significance to the words God speaks and the interchange between God and humanity. So narrative theology guides us away from the act of separating God's actions and words and toward viewing them as being interrelated.

Narrative theology is, compared to other types of theology, constructed around a fuller and more robust idea of God that comes from his enduring, unfolding drama. Juxtaposed to reducing ideas and concepts of God into clean and effortlessly understood categories or propositions, narrative theology is a broad but accurate and pointed construct of God that's more messy than clean and requires more effort to form abstract thoughts about God. Narrative theology finds its meaning in stories, knowing that humans are people of story—God's Story. As Van Engen writes, "Systematic theology engages the intellect; storytelling engages the heart and indeed the whole person."[13]

Too often, enthusiastic and hurried youth workers lead students in an intellectual game of leapfrog from the Story of God directly into the propositions of God, thereby missing the most important aspect of theology altogether—how we allow it to shape and direct our lives. Such leaping creates a hole that some students will never have the opportunity to fill. Before you can legitimize proposition, you have to first legitimize story. Propositions are found throughout the Bible. However, it's sloppy theology to examine propositions without first finding their meaning within the Story itself. Therefore, in order to most effectively and efficiently guide students into Christian formation, we must first consider the greater context in which the propositions are found.

In the following chapter, I'll lead you through an exercise that allows you to consider this greater context. Obviously only a summary of God's narrative, the next chapter still allows us to take a step back, widen the lens, and begin identifying various propositions—all of which have a greater context and meaning.

The Risks and Rewards Associated with Narrative Theology

Several years ago I was in Southeast Asia to attend a meeting of leaders from various youth ministry organizations from around the globe. During one of our sessions, one leader said, "I think we should just teach from the Gospels. Any other text that we teach from just confuses kids." I couldn't believe what I'd heard. I was floored that anyone could make such a statement. Unfortunately, as I've traveled to various places since then, I've found that while people rarely say it as boldly as that gentleman did, they still function that way and most youth ministries are almost exclusively teaching Jesus through the lens of the Gospel narratives. That kind of teaching isn't narrative theology. Narrative theology, like any story, brings context and meaning. Without the greater story, there's no context of who Jesus is; therefore, there's certainly no meaning of Jesus being thrust into the character of a student.

I believe systematic theology, as with most theological constructs, can be helpful. However, I don't believe that a systematic theology that is void of its true narrative context is the best place to start a comprehensive and inclusive study of God.[14] When we start with systematic theology, we may encounter the following hazards.

- We risk missing God's mission to restore the world, as revealed through his interrelated, overarching metanarrative.

- We risk being tempted to contrive concepts of God just to fit them into neat, clean, and easily understood divisions.

- We risk missing the global and local context(s) in which Scripture is given to us and in which it's best understood.

- We risk missing what theologians and scholars throughout history have said about God and led others to believe.

- We risk being closed-minded and therefore afraid of new discoveries and concepts about God that come with a harmonious open-mindedness and imagination.

- We risk simply indoctrinating ourselves and our students with information about God, instead of providing experiential or applied theology that leads to a Christian formation and union with God.

- We risk avoiding the application of God's truths to our modern-day social issues and concerns, which therefore are found by many to be irrelevant.

Therefore, I believe it makes more sense and has a much greater impact when we look at God through the lens of narrative theology. When we do so, we're bound to find the following rewards:

- The unity of the narrative—The parts of God's Story are interrelated and interconnected, thus we find unity in God's entire Story. We don't find meaning in Jesus or the gospel or Pentecost or the flood or the Tower of Babel or the crossing of the Red Sea or any narrative unless we view it in relationship to all of the narratives.

- The universalism of the narrative—Just as the various narratives connect to give meaning to a greater whole, so the narrative provides history for a larger context. The Bible wasn't written for one particular faith heritage or group of people. The Bible was written for all people and for all times, and this makes it unequivocally universal.

- The uncovering of God within the narrative—It's in the unity and universalism of God's narrative that we see the most of God. In the Bible we see the overarching idea and makeup of God, as well as the mighty acts of God. These mighty acts reveal God as a God of power, strength, faithfulness, and so on. It's in the unity of the narrative and its universalism, then, that we see God's mighty work displayed in Jesus.

- The uncovering of the Christ-centered nature of the narrative— Without Jesus, the Story of God remains just as incomprehensible as Jesus would be without God. Jesus Christ is the whole point of the Story. Jesus and the restorative actions of his person and work are in fact the open secret of God.[15] This "open secret" is available to any who wish to welcome it, yet it's a secret to those who don't know about Jesus. This is why God's missionary heart needs to be revealed through the work of God's mission.

The Metanarrative Myth

Postmodernism seems to reject the idea of a metanarrative, among other things. In his book *Bible and Mission: Christian Witness in a Postmodern World*, Richard Bauckham says, "Postmodernism, as defined by Lyotard and others, is rejection of all metanarratives, because, as it attempts to universalize one's own values and culture, they are necessarily authoritarian or oppressive."[16] Postmodernism not only stands in the face of modern metanarratives, but it also works hard to disprove the overarching stories of Christianity and other religions. So if we live in a postmodern context, how does starting with a narrative approach to youth ministry make sense? In other words, if kids today are postmodern and therefore reject the metanarrative because of its oppressive and rationalistic overtones, then what makes us think a narrative approach to youth ministry will work?

Those are really good questions, and I believe they merit taking a moment to explain what I simply refer to as "the metanarrative myth."

Without a doubt postmodernism and the people living in the characteristics of its composition clearly reject anything that puts forth an ideal of impe-rialism. To postmoderns, building an empire for the sake of progress or achievement is in direct conflict with their very beings. You might recognize this feeling of disgust among your students. It's very real, and it's becoming increasingly real every day and in all contexts, be it urban, suburban, or rural. Anything that even sniffs of mastery or dominance is quickly rejected. Postmodernists are much more interested in particularity, diversity, local-ism, and relativism than they are in the idea of one overarching story that provides the meaning of life for all people for all times.[17]

However, when it comes to the biblical story of the metanarrative, depend-ing on the explanation and their interaction with it, postmodernists are gen-erally open to the narrative of God for several reasons. One is that the Bible doesn't have just one storyline. Sure, it has a larger context in which we can view God. But because the Bible isn't a novel and it's filled with differing perspectives of the same stories, specific and smaller stories inside of bigger and less-exacting stories, stories left unfinished, ambivalence in the meaning of certain stories, fragmented stories, and so on, postmodernists are open to seeing the Bible as an accessible and acceptable metanarrative.[18]

These are the words of Richard Bauckham on what I describe as the metanarrative myth, "The Bible does, in some sense, tell an overall story that encompasses all its other contents, but this story isn't a straitjacket that reduces all else to a narrowly defined uniformity."[19]

Just as I'm not an expert in theology, I'm not an expert in postmodernity either. However, I've had enough experience with helping postmodern students meet God through the wider lens of the entire narrative that I can tell you this: Postmodern students will be receptive to the Story of God when it's presented in a way that's hospitable and takes into consideration the ideals of postmodernity. The rejection of the metanarrative is very real for postmodern students. However, we aren't merely working with a story. We're working with a Story filled with theology that reveals who God is in mysterious and complicated ways. For example, Lesslie Newbigin writes, "Whereas the point of the story only becomes clear at its end, the biblical story reveals the point of the whole human story even before its end has been reached."[20] Is that postmodern or what?

THE POSTMODERNIZING OF TRUTH

Along with the rejection of most metanarratives, the postmodernist also rejects absolute truth. This characteristic of postmodernism has been freaking out the church for some time. For nearly all of the years that I've been in youth work, parents and church leaders have been anxiously asking questions about absolute truth and the deterioration of it.

Richard Bauckham writes, "For postmodernists, any claim to universal truth is oppressive because it delegitimizes difference."[21] I agree with that statement. However, I've found that the postmodern students whom I've been in a relationship with aren't really rejecting universal or absolute truth. What most students are rejecting is the way that a particular universal truth is being claimed and presented. Perhaps youth workers (parents, pastors, and so on) shouldn't be so quick to point out a rejection of absolute truth and instead point at themselves as one of the possible primary causes for such rejection.

When truth is presented as being closed and therefore established, most students will reject it. However, when truths about God that we might call "absolute" are presented in a manner worthy of conversation that values the student and their ideals, most students will engage it. At least that's been my experience. If truth is left open for conversation and even skepticism, then there's an open possibility that students will consider it as true and consider it for their own lives.

Furthermore, when things of God are claimed in the same ways that science is claimed, they will be rejected as truth. Science has its own way of verifying the absoluteness of its data. However, Christianity and believers' claims will be received when we're living examples of the things we claim. In other words, when the "data" of our lives and the "data" of our claims match, our students will be receptive.

When presenting the truths we so doggedly believe, it's important to remember to (1) leave conversations about truth open; (2) be sure that before we ever proclaim something to be true, we're living it out; and (3) not try to convince students through the art of persuasion. Within the context of Scripture, reason, and tradition, truth is believed through experience, not through imposition.

When presented appropriately, the narrative of God will evoke the imagination and provide the experience needed to believe. Charles Van Engen writes, "Human beings need story, symbol, image, myth and fiction to disclose to their imaginations some genuinely new possibilities for existence: possibilities which conceptual analysis, committed as it is to understanding present actualities, cannot adequately provide."[22]

FROM NARRATIVE TO MISSION

Mission comes out of one place—God's heart. Mission is an attribute of God that's best understood from God's narrative. God is a missionary God, and therefore mission must be seen as God's movement into the world. That's the exact opposite of how it's often viewed, which is that mission is the primary activity of the church.[23] David Bosch writes, "There is church because there is mission, not vice versa."[24] Of course the church plays a huge role in the mission of God, but the mission of God isn't something the church does; it's simply who God is. Our work is to join God in carrying out his mission, not manufacture our own mission.

Chris Wright, author of *The Mission of God: Unlocking the Bible's Grand Narrative*, says, "Fundamentally, our mission (if it is biblically informed and validated) means our committed participation as God's people, at God's invitation and command, in God's own mission within the history of God's world for the redemption of God's creation."[25] It can be understood from Wright's definition of *mission*, therefore, that youth ministry is our attempt through God's design for the church to participate in God's mission to restore the world.

Youth ministry is about a lot of things, as I'm sure you're well aware. It's about relationships, evangelism, Christian formation, leadership development, justice, and so on. But it's all for the same cause—the redemption of humanity and the restoration of all of God's creation. Therefore, youth workers function as agents of God's restoration, bringing salvation and healing to a lost and broken world.

Mission is important to youth workers for several reasons. First, the mission of God gives us a reason. Sometimes we can get lost in the details of all that we do, and it's easy to take our eyes off God and put them on the things surrounding us.

Second, the mission of God is important to youth workers because it gives both focus and purpose to youth ministry. We aren't needed to be people of our own dreams. Our dreams and our desires to see those dreams accomplished are far from wrong. However, at the end of the day, we do youth ministry because God is a missionary God who longs to see the world he created as "very good" return to its intended condition of wholeness—that's God's dream.

Third, mission work is God's. Remembering this fact takes the pressure off of us. We shouldn't become complacent, but the world isn't ours to win—it's God's. And God does use us to win the world. Nevertheless, we don't conquer the world and lay it at God's feet, saying, "Look what we've done for you!" Rather, we ought to lay *ourselves* at God's feet and say, "Look at what you've done for me, with me, and through me."

Fourth, the mission of God is important to youth workers because it provides the framework in which we view God's activity. We'll talk more about this later on in this chapter. But in short, we don't scurry around and look for ways to structure a ministry platform out of nothing. We look to God—through his narrative—to see a mission that's already at work. Therefore, we aren't needed to "drum up business" for the mission, but rather find where God is already working and join him there.

Finally, the mission of God is important because the mission is the message. In other words, the mission of God articulates the good news that God is a God-for-people.[26] One of the most important aspects of mission is evangelism—proclaiming Jesus Christ as Savior. The proclamation of salvation—or what I refer to as the message of the mission—calls students to repentance and conversion. It calls students to receive or take hold of God's forgiveness, become members of a new community, and begin a life of ministry in the way of Jesus that's powered by and through the Holy Spirit. Youth workers need not worry about creating a message—the message of the mission is already here. And this truth allows you to be creative in other areas.

It's important to remember that the practice of the mission is carried out in a broken world. The message of the mission is simple, but that doesn't mean it's easy. We live in the tension between God's purpose, plan, and providence and humanity's confusion, doubt, and uncertainty. It's important to not only recognize that tension, but also live in it with certainty and calm, knowing that out of an informed balance we bring the message of the mission to our students, and God's compassionate work of the Holy Spirit will do the rest.

Four Ps of God's Mission

Lesslie Newbigin was a theologian and missiologist. While spending many years in India as a missionary, Newbigin was heavily involved in helping people understand God's mission through his teaching and writing. *The Open Secret: An Introduction to the Theology of Mission* was just one of his many works that concisely outlined the mission of God and the message of it in the culture. To Newbigin, the mission is about God *proclaiming* the kingdom, Jesus making the kingdom *present* among God's people, and the *prevenience* (previousness) of the kingdom through the Holy Spirit. In other words, the mission of God forms the context of the person and work of Jesus. Jesus reveals the mission of God to the world through his life, teachings, and deeds.[27] Jesus also sends the Spirit to give witness to the mission of God and to equip the church for its mission to participate with God in restoring the world to its intended wholeness.

Newbigin gives three "P" words to help us understand the mission of God: *Proclaim*, *present*, and *prevenience*. I'd like to add a fourth: *Practice*. *Story, Signs, and Sacred Rhythms* is about helping you establish a framework in which to carry out the mission of God. The Holy Spirit equips the church to practice the work of God or to live out the Story of God—and our youth ministries need to be about the practice of the mission.

But before we can begin with a comprehensive framework for narrative-missional youth ministry, it's important that we understand the origin, nature, work, and goals of the mission of God. Youth ministry that's living out the heart of God through its missionary activity must deeply realize the correlation between God's mission and the work of our youth ministries.

The Origins of the Mission of God

We've already established this; but for the sake of review, the mission of God finds its origin in the heart of God. In the words of David Bosch, in *Transforming Mission*:

> It cannot be denied that the missio Dei notion has helped to articulate the conviction that neither the church nor any other human agent can ever be considered the author or bearer of mission. Mission is, primarily and ultimately, the work of the Triune God, Creator, Redeemer, and Sanctifier, for the sake of the world, a ministry in which the church is privileged to participate...Mission has its origin in the heart of God. God is a fountain of sending love. This is the deepest source of mission. It is impossible to penetrate deeper still; there is mission because God loves people.[28]

We aren't about our own work. We're exclusively about the work of God—as seen in his heart, through his mission, and understood best from his narrative. The origin of mission has its source in the heart of God, not our church bulletins, Web sites, or mission statements, which are often based on one verse or proposition. While it's important to contextualize the mission of God, we must keep in mind that the more we try to reduce God into understandable, incremental propositions for our students, the smaller God becomes. And the smaller God becomes, the fewer reasons our students have to accept and then contribute to God's mission of salvation and justice.

I appreciate the words of Charles Van Engen:

> Mission is the people of God intentionally crossing barriers
>
> from church to nonchurch, faith to nonfaith,
>
> to proclaim by word and deed
>
> the coming of the kingdom of God in Jesus Christ;

this task is achieved by means of the church's participation in God's mission

of reconciling people to God, to themselves, to each other, and to the world,

and gathering them into the church through repentance and faith in Jesus Christ

by the work of the Holy Spirit

with a view to the transformation of the world

as a sign of the coming kingdom in Jesus Christ.[29]

The Nature of the Mission of God

There are three integrative aspects of the nature of the mission of God that must be understood: The *biblical text*, the people of God or *faith communities*, and the *cultural context* in which our individual faith communities and the biblical text intersect—our missional context.[30] Each of these is imperative to the mission of God and the work that our youth ministries do to complete God's mission. Regardless of the model of ministry, the work of the church (and therefore youth ministry) is to integrate the culture, the Bible, and the faith community and ultimately express the heart of God— to save the world and bring justice to all.

At times it's hard to remember that we don't do youth ministry outside of the culture. For many of us, there's an urge to protect our kids from it. Sure, we want the culture to interact with our faith community—we call this "outreach." I contend, however, that culture is just as much a part of the mission of God as is the faith community—even as much as Scripture is. In other words, if the nature of the mission of God involves all three, then why do we tend to separate culture from the Bible and the faith community? Youth ministry must work diligently to integrate all three.

must integrate culture, bible, & faith community

The Work of the Mission of God

We're going to look at the work of God's mission in greater detail in a later chapter. However, for our purpose of providing a concise summation of the

mission of God, I believe it's important for us to realize there are traditionally four key components of the work we do to carry out God's mission.

We're about *evangelism* or proclaiming and performing the message of the
mission. We're about the *contextualization* of the message of the mission,
which we'll continue to discuss throughout this book. The work of the mission of God is *liberation*. Our youth ministries must be about setting people
free from the constraints that keep them from establishing a restorative
relationship with God, themselves, others, and the world. The work of
youth ministry is about freeing students from the very things that hold
them captive.[31] And the work of proclaiming the message of the mission
is to *impart* the mission into the culture. This isn't a mere contextualization
where the mission is made relevantly accessible. Rather, it's about convert-
ing the culture from hearers to storytellers of the mission of God.

To jump back to the nature of the mission for a second, this proves how
important the culture is to the mission of God and why it can arguably be
considered equal to the roles of Scripture and faith communities. If there's
no culture, then there's no need to impart the message of the mission. If
there's no culture, then to whom are we proclaiming the message of the
mission?

*[handwritten annotation: Four key components to the work we do (see above)
1. Evangelism   4. Impart
2. Contextualization
3. Liberation]*

The Goals of the Mission of God

There are two primary goals of the mission of God, and I've alluded to
them already. The two goals of God's mission are *salvation* and *justice*.
According to Millard Erickson, in his book *Christian Theology*, "salvation is a
total change in an individual that progresses through sanctification toward
glorification."[32] Traditionally, salvation involves regeneration, sanctification,
adoption, justification, redemption, reconciliation, and union. Out of these
important components, we're able to see signs of new life.[33] What do those
signs look like? They include—

- Finding fellowship with God and his people

- A love for God and his people

- The proclamation of Jesus as a means of delivering the message
  of the mission of God

- Ongoing obedience to the intended ways of God and teachings
  of Scripture

- Trying to do the will of God

- Yielding to the work and ministry of the Holy Spirit in us and through us.

Our youth ministries are clearly about the work of salvation, but they should also be about the work of justice.

Simply said, the work of justice is righting wrongs.[34] While salvation does provide justice in a larger, more comprehensive way, our youth ministries aren't solely about saving souls. In fact, I believe we fall short of God's intended mission to restore the world to its intended wholeness when our agenda contains only the salvation of the soul. We ought to also be about righting the wrongs in our world—bringing a true dignity to all.

The mission of God places us directly in the heart of a broken world where we're to look for ways to care for the physical, emotional, and social needs of those around us just as much as we're to care for their spiritual needs. Regardless of the outcome of our acts of deep justice, when we care for God's people and God's creation, we warm the missionary heart of God.

It isn't evangelism or justice—it's *both*. They may be separated in task and function at times, but they're never two separate, optional components of the mission of God.

As you know, there are various essential aspects of social concern and justice. In talking with my Catholic youth worker friends, I've discovered that the Catholic Church designates seven areas or key themes related to justice (as identified by the United States Conference of Catholic Bishops). Those themes are—

1. Sanctity of human life and dignity of the person

2. Call to family, community, and participation

3. Rights and responsibilities [of humanity]

4. Preferential [care] for the poor and vulnerable

5. Dignity of work and the rights of workers

6. Solidarity

7. Care for God's creation[35]

I believe each of our youth ministries could measure its efforts and effectiveness in the areas of social concern and justice around these seven key themes. In doing so, I believe we could more deeply engage the mission of God specifically to the integration of the Scriptures, the context of our faith communities, and the context of the surrounding culture. And as a result of our growing awareness of areas of concern and ongoing acts of compassion, perhaps we might see the righting of wrongs in such areas as violence elimination, ecology, politics, income redistribution, racial equality, healthcare, urban and rural renewal, fair trade, and an end to modern-day slavery.

For our youth ministries to be about justice, we leaders must first seek to examine our own hearts. Are we compassionate people? Do we care about justice? Why do we care about justice? An examination of the heart will most often lead to a confession of neglect. We recognize the importance of justice, but we often leave it for others to do. Neglect is far too common. Look around you. You'll see people in need today—and not just halfway around the world but halfway down your block.

But people in need aren't just financially poor and in need of food, money, and clothes. Poverty-stricken people may also be those who need love, respect, care, and friendship. There are people living in my neighborhood who are poor. They may live in 3,000 square foot homes and have all the money they need, but without love in their lives, they're poor. We need to examine our hearts not only for compassion, but also for respect toward the people we choose to be compassionate to and with.

For our youth ministries to be about justice (along with salvation), we must repent of our neglect just as we'd repent of other sins. We must also begin to stand with the undignified and exploited of this world. It isn't enough for our youth ministry and students to just do acts of service. We must seek active justice by living amid the needs of others.

In *A Glimpse of Jesus: The Stranger to Self-Hatred*, Brennan Manning quotes Barbara Doherty:

> Love is service. There is no point in getting into an argument about this question of loving. It is what Christianity is all about— take it or leave it. Christianity is not about ritual and moral living except insofar as these two express the love that causes both of them. We must at least pray for the grace to become love.[36]

The narrative of God reveals the mission of God. The mission of God reveals the very heart of God. It's through God's heart of love that the work of our youth ministries becomes increasingly clear and incredibly compelling. We're to be about the salvation and justice of this world, as determined by God and through the efforts of evangelism, contextualization, liberation, and impartation. The rest of this book will concern itself with helping you grasp the larger Story of God and, out of that, constructing a narrative approach to youth ministry—an approach that's sourced by the heart of God and resourced by the person and work of Jesus and the ministry of the Holy Spirit.

Reflection and Discussion Questions
Chapter 2—Narrative and Mission

• What does it mean for today's church to be thought of as "pilgrim people" or people "on the way"?

• Do you agree with the statement: "It's sloppy theology to examine propositions without first finding their meaning within the Story itself"? Why or why not?

• Do you believe teaching with a full narrative view of Jesus confuses students? Why or why not?

• Would you say your students are postmodern? Why or why not?

• Are you concerned about the apparent deterioration of truth? Why or why not?

• Do you agree with the statement: "Truth is believed through experience, not through imposition"? Why or why not?

• If you were to describe God's dream for the world, how might you describe it?

• Do you agree with the statement: "Culture is just as much a part of the mission of God as is the faith community, or even Scripture"? Why or why not?

- In what ways is your youth ministry going about the work of God's mission—salvation and justice?

- How might we hold each other accountable to avoiding the neglect of those in need?

PART ONE: STORY

I believe we live in a narratable world, meaning, we live in a world filled with stories of God, self, others, and the surrounding world. While Christians believe God is the storyteller of the overarching story or metanarrative of this world, others may place their belief more in the micro-stories of self and others around them. Regardless, it's clear that stories are central to our understanding of ourselves and the world we live in.

It's widely understood that any story has three primary external elements—storyteller, story, and audience. These external components aren't to be confused with the highly important internal components that make up a story, such as plot, character development, conflict, setting, point of view, and so on. Rather, the nature and interaction of these three external elements are the very things that produce the internal elements. The Bible is like this. It has various stories filled with plot, characters, setting, and so on. But these stories are all within the context of the storytelling triangle of Storyteller (God), Story, and audience.[37]

Throughout this section on Story, we'll look at God as *Storyteller*, the *stories* God has weaved together, and the *people* to whom God is telling this unfolding, enduring narrative. Grasping each of these three components of the Story of God is essential to our overall understanding of the missionary heart of God, the mission of God, and the role of humanity in the mission of God. God is the Storyteller who tells the Story of his amazing love, grace, and mercy. God's Story reveals his missionary heart. And it's in seeing into God's heart that we find the nature of our existence.

In his book *Experiential Storytelling: (Re)Discovering Narrative to Communicate God's Message*, my friend Mark Miller writes:

> We were created with a curiosity, a complexity, and a need for meaning. That longing to understand the bigger questions is a deep need that cannot be filled with mere facts. God did not choose to reveal a list of facts to us. The Old Testament was given to humanity in the form of narratives and poetry. Even the writing of the law took place in the midst of the deeply compelling story of God redeeming his chosen people.[38]

Miller is talking about these same three components of story within the Story of God. First, God as the Storyteller is the One who fills our curiosity, complexity, and meaning; and it's filled with image, mission, and work.

Second, it's the narrative that God tells and the stories God continues to write in which we're such a valuable and vital part that we find context and meaning for who we're called to be. Finally, it's the "compelling" Story of God redeeming his people in which we, the audience of this great Story of God, reside.

Another common aspect of all of our stories is their interconnectedness. One form of connection is through chronological time. Our stories connect us to the past, giving us history. They connect us with the present, giving us meaning and context. Our stories, however unique to us, give us a sense of purpose for all of life and connect us to God's future.

Our stories also connect us sociologically to communities of people. If we're connected to history—past, present, and future—then we're also connected to humanity in the same ways—as it was, as it is now, and what's inevitably yet to come.

And we're connected sociologically because we're first connected theologically. God has given us a Story—the Bible—in which to understand the relationships between God, ourselves, and others.

In *Tell Me a Story: The Life-Shaping Power of Our Stories*, Daniel Taylor writes, "Seeing our lives as stories, rather than as an unrelated series of random events, increases the possibility for having in our own lives what we find best in the stories: significant, purposeful action."[39] God allows us to see our lives as a connected story within his grand Story. This is what all of us want—connectedness and the knowledge that what we're here to do matters deeply to the outcomes of this world. If nothing in the world changes for the better because we've lived and breathed, then it becomes difficult to find our reason to live.

Our students need to know that their lives are interwoven over time (past, present, and future) into a purposeful plot.[40] Plot comes out of a story, told or woven, by a storyteller who has a purpose for his audience. As Henri Nouwen said, "People want to see and hear stories and experience their own stories in the context of a larger, more dramatic, more explicit, or more intense one."[41]

This is what the narrative and mission of God does for us: It provides us with a larger, more dramatic, more explicit, and more intense story in which we find God, ourselves, our relationships with others, and the surrounding world. It's through this Story of God, which I believe serves as a history book for all of humanity, that we're introduced to Jesus and caught up into his way of life. It's from within stories of the Story that we see God's mission to restore the world to its intended wholeness and our role in it as modeled by the One the Story of God serves, Jesus.

CHAPTER 3

Preparation: God's Story as the Context for Discovering God's Mission

Before we look more specifically at the proposed model for youth ministry that I've outlined in this book, I believe it will prove itself fundamental to set up the ideas, concepts, stories, and so on, by taking a foundational, yet reflective look into the great Story of God.

For many of you, this chapter will be completely review. There's a very real chance that many of you have spent a great deal of time over the last several years studying, listening to, meditating upon, and living out the Story as arranged below.

Nevertheless, I encourage you not to skip over or carelessly skim this section of the book in order to get to the "good stuff" that you assume will be of "greater" help to you as you think about your ministry to students and their families. If nothing else, take the next few minutes simply to be affirmed in the implementation of your current philosophy of youth ministry, measuring your efforts against the heart and desires of God. It's a big undertaking, but essential nonetheless.

Entering into the next several pages of this book with a receptive heart and a willing spirit will help you more fully engage in the rest of the book.

A PREPARATORY LOOK AT THE NARRATIVE OF GOD

The narrative of God and the unfolding, accessible drama found within the beauty and mystery of its poetry, songs, letters, and prophecy brings us heart-to-heart with God. Worshipped by awestruck people from the beginning of creation and time, God, through his Story, gives us a convincing proposal as to who God is, why God designed creation in certain ways, and what God's creation is to be and become. It's out of discovery, exploration, and an ongoing experience with God's narrative that Christians are able to remain increasingly convinced of God's being, reign, presence, and activity in the world.

God has the ability to introduce his personhood to the various stages of generations gone by (as well as those yet to come) in any way he wishes. Thus, God deliberately and voluntarily revealed his will, his way, and his work for humanity through what the world commonly refers to as the Bible—God's Story. The Bible has long been the one thing that humanity has held on to as a sacred work of God—a work that supplies his fearers and hearers with a window into the supernatural, steadfast, and eternal being of God.

When we align the major movements of God's Story with God's purpose, character, and priorities, we begin to identify with his wide range of attributes, such as life, grace, justice, mercy, jealousy, anger, hope, and expectancy. These qualities provide us with an awareness of God's existence and presence as we experience him more deeply every day.

An introduction into the major movements of God is a great starting point for not only discovering God, but also learning to live within the framework of his will, way, and work for each of our lives. Before we can really embrace God as the Creator and Ruler of the kingdom in which we take up residence and allow God to govern our being, we must understand more clearly (and become increasingly tied to) the Story of God.

It's not enough for us to just know stories *about* God. Instead, we must know and begin to lean into and live out the Story *of* God—and so must the students within our reach. Furthermore, we must understand the missio Dei (mission of God) that's found within the narrative. (This refers to the particular purpose and plan that God has for drawing people—or better yet, *restoring* people—to what was once a good, right, and whole relationship with him.)

God is actively pursuing a restored relationship with humanity. He desires that one day the relationship with his creation be restored to its intended wholeness. We can better appreciate and understand God's original condition, his original intent, and his unceasing restorative activity through the major movements of his narrative and the observations and reflections we make regarding those movements.

One way to explore the major movements of God is in the form of a storyboard—a succession of panels arranged in progressive order to more clearly depict the actions to be viewed. This storyboard is my brief and limited attempt at helping you focus on God's great Story before you launch into the practical, executable functions of this book. I know you want a model for ministry—and we'll get there, I promise. Just as I contend that a student can't have a full and robust context and meaning for who Jesus is without having first had a deep and engaging interaction with God's overarching Story, I also believe you won't be able to implement the model put forth in this book (or any other model, for that matter) without making the time to marinate in and be preserved by the narrative of God.

As with any summation, the following summary of the major movements in the activity of God has its limitations. I confess that the big picture of God's Story cannot be completely summarized in seven movements or episodes. Therefore, the storyboard summation to follow is simply an attempt to help us view the mission of God through the widest lens possible as we seek to guide students into Christian formation for the purpose of the missio Dei.

It's also important to note here that these seven movements or episodes aren't intended to represent certain dispensations of the faith. Instead, the movements are simply designed to represent the various parts of a greater whole or the micronarratives found within the metanarrative.

With that in mind, let's review what many of us already know about the major movements of God's Story using a simple but helpful storyboard concept. I invite you to interact with this process by utilizing the sidebar panels and reflection questions. In each blank panel, record something that will remind you of the Story and help you remember the truths found in each movement. The reminder may be a symbol, a few phrases or key words, or another artistic interpretation. It can be different for every panel. Then take some time to answer the personal reflection questions found at the bottom of each sidebar. You can either utilize the sidebars as you read each panel, or you can return to the sidebars when you've finished reading all of the panels. Do whatever works best for you, but take your time, marinate in God's Story, and let it enliven you as it preserves you in God's great embrace.

Panel 1—The Creation Movement

God existed alone, it would appear. However, in God's unaccompanied being there was triunity between God as Father, God as Son, and God as Holy Spirit. The divine activity surrounding the Creation Movement reveals to us how everything we've come to know (and all that we have yet to know) came to be. However, it still keeps us guessing when it comes to the mystery and theories surrounding the always-existent Creator.

We conclude that God was alone and he designed everything from nothing. Theologians call this *ex nihilo*, meaning that God simply spoke all that we've come to know into being. Life and all that it includes and all that encircles it is the truly inexplicable work of a God who imaginatively, out of nothing but his own brainstorm, created light, water, air, earth, plants, animals, and humans.

Sometimes viewed as the most important aspect of God's design, humans were the basis for community and the relationships between groups of people and God. It was out of an incredibly artistic and intelligent design that humanity was formed to be the structure of relationship—of family. And from out of the intimacy of family emerges the immensity of many nations.

As individuals who've been created in the "image" or "likeness" of God, we've been given intellect, emotion, and will. And not apart from those three essentials of intelligent life, we've also been created to be a representation of God and his intended will, way, and work of life.

Panel 1—The Creation Movement

God created in His image in perfect unison w/ Him.

Personal Reflection

• *What does this movement of God's activity help you to learn or remember about God?*
He created us for His glory.

• *What does this movement of God's activity help you to learn or remember about humanity?* *We were created for a purpose.*

• *How does what you're learning or remembering about the movements of God's activity shape your theology?*
That God works to love us and for us to love back.

In reflection of the Trinity, then, people were created to be a living portrayal of God's nature. Humans were created to be *eikons* (or "icons") of God. We're created to care for and protect all that God gave to us; live in community as one family; and illustrate the meaning, matchlessness, and majesty of God. Therefore, as humans we hold inherent value, demonstrate distinctiveness, and display dignity.

The Creation Movement begins out of nothing and ends with the declaration that all that God has designed is good—very good, in fact. God and humans were in a completely harmonious relationship.

Panel 2—The Crisis Movement

Since God created humans with the ability to reason, God also allowed humans to make choices. Although sin wasn't a new idea to God (think Lucifer and the account of his separation from God in Ezekiel 28:11-19 and Isaiah 14:12-14), God gave humanity enough information and knowledge about what sin could and couldn't do to allow us to make an informed decision. Yet, humanity chose to rebel and was therefore no longer in good standing within the family. The once harmonious relationship between God and humans was shattered.

The consequences of this broken relationship soon became very apparent: Shame, suffering, toil, pain, decay, and erosion of the soul became the unwanted but explicit rudiments of a broken relationship. And this broken relationship wasn't confined to the relationship between God and humans, either. Rather, this brokenness was evidenced in how humans now viewed themselves, how they related to one another, and even in the entirety of God's creation.

God already knew the pain of being separated from his creation (again, think Lucifer). But what he hadn't apparently experienced yet was the feeling of being wounded a second time. When humanity rebelled, it was a second series of pain. Fortunately for humanity, God—in his infinite grace and mercy—decided not to become calloused by the second sting of sin, but chose to reach deep into his being and bestow a canopy of love so big that it sheltered the entire creation.

This canopy—a flood of love, if you will—reached the outermost

---

Panel 2—The Crisis Movement

Oh No! Where did God go?

Personal Reflection

• *What does this movement of God's activity help you to learn or remember about God?*
He is graciouss, and we are only whole with Him.

• *What does this movement of God's activity help you to learn or remember about humanity?* That we are all separated from Him.

• *How does what you're learning or remembering about the movements of God's activity shape your theology?*
God is loving and graciouss

points possible. With the exception of a righteous man named Noah, some members of Noah's family, and a good number of animals, God cleansed the entire earth of the wickedness, debauchery, decay, and erosion of the soul—the worst kind of erosion.

Panel 3—The Promise Movement

In the same imaginative way that God created humans and all the rest, God gives special attention to providing a path away from our brokenness and separation. God gives humanity the opportunity to once again live in harmony with him. Of course, this pathway is much different from the one he originally sketched, but nevertheless a promise was made.

God spoke a promise to Abram (later named Abraham), and that promise indicated that God would make Abraham into a great nation—a blessed nation chosen by God to emerge out of obscurity and into the brightness of fulfillment. God chose Abraham and his descendants to be the pathway or agent of restoration—*salvation*. This great nation was to be not only a blessed nation, but also a nation that might serve as a blessing to others—through *justice*.

This promise of God is imperative to his character and mission and to our grasp of God's mission. If one cannot work to trust the great nation of Abraham and the new pathway toward the restoration of God and humanity, then the entire narrative falls onto not only deaf ears, but also numb souls. For it's out of this great promise that God wills his people—who

Panel 3—The Promise Movement

Abraham gets a shot at restoration.

Personal Reflection

• *What does this movement of God's activity help you to learn or remember about God?*
God uses people

• *What does this movement of God's activity help you to learn or remember about humanity?* *That we are still faulty.*

• *How does what you're learning or remembering about the movements of God's activity shape your theology?*
He Has a plan

were created in his image—to be a vital part of his unending restorative activity.

Panel 4—The Movement of God's People, Part 1

By providing land, laws, and leaders—and all for the purpose of pointing people to Jesus—God continues fulfilling his promise to the world. Through Abraham's son Isaac, Jacob, Joseph, Moses, Miriam, Deborah, Joshua, Samuel, Saul, David, and a host of other key individuals, God's people emerge into the kingdom where they were intended to be.

Panel 4—The Movement of God's People, Part 1

Israel was supposed to be Showing God to the world. Which they did at times, however they were not very good at it.

Personal Reflection

• *What does this movement of God's activity help you to learn or remember about God?*

God is working on restoring.

• *What does this movement of God's activity help you to learn or remember about humanity?* *Humanity is flawed.*

• *How does what you're learning or remembering about the movements of God's activity shape your theology?*

He is Sovereign.

But in keeping with the nature of humanity and its rebellious patterns, the kingdom divides into the northern (Israel) and the southern (Judah) kingdoms. Both are oppressed by other nations and its people are placed into slavery.

Under the leadership of Zerubbabel, Ezra, and Nehemiah (along with the presence and direction of God), the temple of God is rebuilt and the focus is again placed on God and his intended ways—the law.

For some 1,500 years, the people of God struggled to remain faithful to God, his way, and his mission to be a blessing to other nations. After promising through the prophets to send someone who would save the nation of Israel, God sat in silence for somewhere close to 400 years. And for 400 years, the people of God who once knew God's presence, care, and protection through clouds, miracles, temple worship, rituals, festivals, practicing the law, and many other symbols no longer experienced the communion with God they'd intermittently treasured up to this point.

Panel 5—The God-With-Us Movement

Out of yet another imaginative act of God, God chooses to dwell with his people for a season of time and in the form of a man named Jesus. Jesus had a message. He had many messages, actually. But the subject he spoke of most often was the kingdom of God.

Through his teachings, miracles, and modeling, Jesus provided a picture of what it looks like to live fully human. Jesus shows humanity what it means to passionately live in such a way that unshakably loves God, loves people, and brings honor to God.

Jesus emphasizes a special concern for those who live in poverty, are considered socially unacceptable, and described as outcasts (such as the paralyzed and the lepers). Jesus also spends a great deal of time healing (the blind, oppressed, bruised, broken, and so on) and teaching his hearers about putting others first.

As Jesus goes about his ministry, he takes the time to invest in a few young men we commonly refer to as the 12 disciples. It's obvious in reading through the Gospels that Jesus was teaching his disciples how to love, live, and lead like he does. Jesus did this so that long after he was gone, the disciples might be able to carry on Christ's mission and create communities

Panel 5—The God-With-Us Movement

Yay! Jesus! He shows us how it's done!

Personal Reflection

• *What does this movement of God's activity help you to learn or remember about God?*
God is personal

• *What does this movement of God's activity help you to learn or remember about humanity?* *We need a saviour*

• *How does what you're learning or remembering about the movements of God's activity shape your theology?*
God will stop at nothing to restore us.

of people who'd also give themselves to God's enduring plan of restoring the world.

Jesus is put to death on a cross. Mockingly, but not coincidentally, Jesus is crowned the "King of the Jews" and publicly dishonored; yet he's also privately honored. Although God had "forsaken" his own Son, deep down beneath the profoundness of the crucifixion events God is delighted with his Son's actions. God's mission continues—just as God said it would—through the events and prophecy found within the history and heritage of the Jewish tradition, and through the birth, life, death, burial, resurrection, and ascension (also known as the "incarnation") of his Son Jesus.

Jesus' incarnation is considered the climax of God's Story. It's out of these events that God provides a pathway into his kingdom, which points us to trusting in Jesus as the way into the kingdom, the way in which to live within the scope of the kingdom, and into the eternal life that allows us to reside in the kingdom.

Panel 6—The Movement of God's People, Part 2

The Church! God help us do your will.

Personal Reflection

• *What does this movement of God's activity help you to learn or remember about God?*
He works through us.

• *What does this movement of God's activity help you to learn or remember about humanity?* *We can be used by God, but we have to humble ourselves.*

• *How does what you're learning or remembering about the movements of God's activity shape your theology?*

Panel 6—The Movement of God's People, Part 2

After Jesus' death, burial, and resurrection, he appears to his friends and family on several different occasions. He spends 40 days convincing his disciples of his resurrection and teaching them about the kingdom. Along with his kingdom teachings, Jesus promises to send the Spirit to guide his people, as they're inspired and empowered to become storytellers or witnesses of God's great storylines. Jesus' teachings about the kingdom, the Holy Spirit, witnesses, and so on all help us to see the restorative plan and activity of God.

Just as Jesus promised, the Holy Spirit presents himself to Jesus' followers, whom we commonly refer to as "the early church," and empowers them with the necessary authority and power to continue in the way of Jesus. Bringing an offering of hope and formation, the Holy Spirit guides the newly formed church as it develops the groundwork for the people of God to follow as the church expands in size and scope in order to reach the outermost, lost, and forgotten parts of the world.

With careful attention to the foundation the Spirit was laying down, the new church community established its priorities as teaching, evangelism, service, justice, community, and worship. After watching Jesus live, love, and lead, the disciples were able to practice key virtues of Jesus. In doing so, they continued to fulfill the mission of Jesus as he'd once described it in Luke chapter 4. This mission of Jesus, as seen in the Scripture below, was a continuation of the mission that God already outlined for Abraham—to be a blessing to other nations.

Here is Jesus describing his mission on earth:

> Jesus returned to Galilee in the power of the Spirit, and news about him spread through the whole countryside. He was teaching in their synagogues, and everyone praised him. He went to Nazareth, where he had been brought up, and on the Sabbath day he went into the synagogue, as was his custom. He stood up to read, and the scroll of the prophet Isaiah was handed to him. Unrolling it, he found the place where it is written: "The Spirit of the Lord is on me, because he has anointed me to proclaim good news to the poor. He has sent me to proclaim freedom for the prisoners and recovery of sight for the blind, to set the oppressed free, to proclaim the year of the Lord's favor." Then he rolled up the scroll, gave it back to the attendant and sat down. The eyes of everyone in the synagogue were fastened on him. He began by saying to them, "Today this scripture is fulfilled in your hearing." (Luke 4:14-21)

Today, the people of God—the church—are helping God write the next chapter in his storyline as we strive to live out the mission of God. Well, we aren't actually writing it; we're more likely *yielding* to it. God is still very much about pursuing humanity. His desire to restore relations with humanity to our intended wholeness hasn't waned. The church worldwide (but especially our local faith communities) is working to be the blessing and love that God foretold we'd be and commanded us to become.

The new community formed after the incarnation of Jesus received the promise, presence, and power of the Holy Spirit. Through the Holy Spirit, the intended way of community life and Christian formation is modeled for us. Our churches and the ministry segments that cooperate with each other, namely youth ministry, are in the process of helping people find God in order that they may be restored.

As the church and our specific faith communities join in the activity of God, we're fulfilling the calling that God placed on his people. We're a continuation of the promise God made to Abraham many thousands of years ago. We're a new community—a new kind of people who are helping to reveal God's will and way and provision of salvation to all of humanity by living out God's Story—making it more than just a legend or myth. We're making it a dependable, authentic, and emerging way of life.

As we live today within this movement, we, the people of God, focus our time on the mission of God, knowing that to live missionally is a simple way to live. It's simple in the sense that our role isn't convoluted and vague. Rather, it's clear and bright. We're to be an illumined people working to bless others.

Panel 7—The Movement of Restoration

God's people look forward to experiencing a sweet reunion with God. While we live with an awareness of God's presence and move about every day while staying united to the aroma of God's love, mercy, patience, goodness, kindness, and grace, we still eagerly await the day that God will choose to dwell with his people once more.

We speculate as to what the future dwelling with God might look like as we draw together a point of view from this movement of God's great Story. As we put forward ideas and concepts around the reality of the future dwelling, we cannot help but imagine a better day. We imagine a day of restoration—of purification, complete healing, jubilation, shared triumph, and an extraordinary sense of wholeness.

The shattered pieces of our lives—and the lives of those we love—are carefully and creatively being restored as we move about God's mission. The future dwelling in and of the presence of God will be the age in which we'll have finally been completely restored. All things will be made new. We'll experience a life we haven't yet conceived of.

Remarkably, and almost unbelievably, God also awaits the day of this future reunion. God looks forward to the day when the "garden" is repopulated. That is, as God restores this world, he's remembering the age of goodness. I believe God longs to reside once more with his people within the boundaries of his intended condition of wholeness for this world.

We'll one day live in harmony with our Author and Creator. God's mission to restore the world will be complete, and his will, way, and work of providing salvation and justice to humanity will be one of the many reasons we'll be faithful to worship him for all of eternity.

Panel 7—The Movement of Restoration

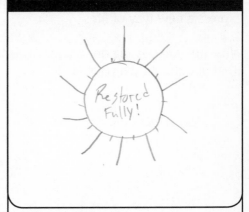

Personal Reflection

• *What does this movement of God's activity help you to learn or remember about God?*
He is in the restoration business.

• *What does this movement of God's activity help you to learn or remember about humanity?* We are meant for something bigger.

• *How does what you're learning or remembering about the movements of God's activity shape your theology?*
God will restore us.

CONTEXT AND MEANING

The Story of God, as we've briefly outlined it in this chapter, helps us more fully understand God. The Story of God is rich and deep. In fact, each time we return to the Story, we see new things. And, as I mentioned earlier, we cannot effectively move forward in this book if we don't take time to remember and reflect on God's amazing Story.

I believe our students need to establish context and meaning for who they are and who they're becoming as followers of Jesus. I also contend that as their shepherd (in partnership with other spiritual influences in their life) you're the one to help them obtain context and meaning. If our students are asking, "Why?" as it relates to understanding the context and meaning of Jesus, then we haven't given them enough to form a deep understanding. And if students don't have a deeper understanding, then they can't express a new way of life.

What are you passing on to your students? Remember, you can't give away what you don't own yourself.

Reflection and Discussion Questions

Chapter 3—Preparation: God's Story as the Context for Discovering God's Mission

- Take a moment to share with your group what you noticed during the Personal Reflection exercises for each Story panel.

- In what ways are you helping your students interact with the entire narrative of God?

- In what ways might you be more creative, innovative, or intentional about helping your students deeply engage with the narrative of God?

- How might what you're learning or remembering about the Movements of God's activity shape your future ministry practices?

CHAPTER 4

Revelation: God's Story as the Context for Our Participation in God's Mission

We seldom talk about revelation in youth ministry. It isn't intentional; it just seems like one of those subjects that's mentioned only occasionally. But I believe we need to talk about revelation a whole lot more.

Revelation is typically understood as the way God has revealed himself to humanity. Theologians typically differentiate God's revelation in two primary ways: *General* revelation and *special* revelation.

General revelation concerns itself with how God can be seen and best understood through creation. This means that in human nature, physical nature, and throughout history we see God in each one of us—no matter what our size, shape, or skin color might be—as well as in the animals, the mountains and lakes, the forests and fields, the ocean waves, the soft sandy beaches, and even in the planets, moon, sun, and stars. God is in everything physical and in everything human. God is in all of life.

Special revelation concerns itself with direct communication from God. The incarnation of Jesus Christ, the Bible, and the assorted divine communications with the prophets—both past and present—are all examples of special revelation. God is in story, as we've already seen. God is also, therefore, in mission.

Scholars can argue about the various ways in which we understand revelation. Some might put forth that revelation is best understood through experience or culture, while others might declare that revelation is best understood through proposition or Scripture. Still others might suggest that God reveals himself through all of the above—experience, culture, proposition, *and* Scripture. I'm sure, like many other fundamentals, humans will debate this issue for centuries to come.

For the purpose of this book, however, I want us to focus on one fact, regardless of the four areas of thought mentioned above. The bottom line is that God has revealed himself to us through a variety of forms, but none is more important than God's narrative—the Bible.

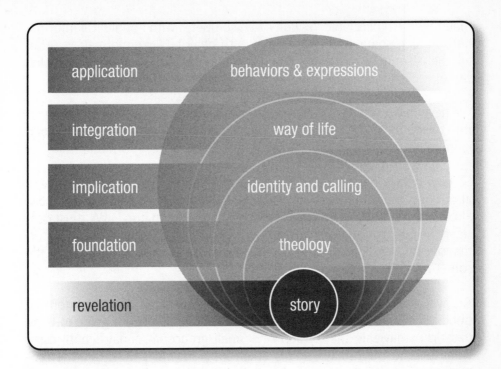

It's from within the narrative of God that we have mission, and it's out of mission that you and I have purpose. As David Bosch has said, "There is church [and youth ministry] because there is mission, not vice versa."[42]

CONCEPTUAL NOISE

Students, just like adults, have cognitive clutter.[43] Clutter is simply a disorderly array of messages that impedes understanding.[44] Students' friends, parents, teachers, coaches, classmates, and youth workers all pump various types of information into their heads and hearts. Some are good, some not so good. Some are godly, some not so much. But regardless of who's delivering whatever kind of information that our students receive, it's all cognitive clutter. This means that students' minds (and ultimately their hearts) are filled with a wide range of competing thoughts and ideas; and therefore, they sometimes lack the necessary clarity to sort out God as he's understood through the Bible.

Although youth leaders work hard to present our students with ideas about God in relevant and helpful ways, for some students it's all competing infor-

mation—the biblical information often competes with nonbiblical information. In fact, sometimes it competes with *other* biblical information. After
all, there's only so much that one can retain and only so much that makes
sense.

We have to do a better job. Quite often, we youth workers are to blame for
the conceptual noise. Therefore, it's my contention that students don't need
more information; they need a better way *through* the information.[45]

So how do we do this? Well, for starters, I believe we need to be careful
about how much information we present. We need to think long and hard
about the methods we use to present the information, too.[46] We must consider the composition of the environments in which we deliver the information. And we should really spend some time thinking harder about the
content we're presenting.

Are we even aware of the content? I mean, how often do we rely on the
publisher's logo? Many of us are just glad to have a leader's guide in hand
to help us navigate the tension of a small group or Sunday school class.
Honestly, most of us have simply taken someone else's word that the content or information we're sharing with our students is worth presenting.
Any way you look at it, we have to do a better job in our pursuit to help students discover and decipher the truth through all of the conceptual noise.
I don't believe that providing more information or trying to speak louder
than other points of influence (friends, parents, media, and so on) is the
way to go.

Like you, I want the students I serve to have as much knowledge about
God and the things of God as humanly possible. I'd love to know that my
students can identify 8 to 10 of the various names of God, speak about just
as many of God's attributes, define the Trinity, explain the covenants, and
so on. Unfortunately, while I believe many students can take all of that in,
most just bat around those concepts with the rest of the conceptual noise
in their head.

Don't fool yourself into believing students are "getting it" just because they
memorize a few verses, occasionally nod in agreement with something you
said, or pass an "exam" of some kind in order to be confirmed. Most students aren't retaining the information you're giving to them. (We'll talk
more in depth about a method for combating this truism in the next chapter.) You might be the best teacher or small group leader or conversational-
ist on the planet. However, like adults, students can only take in and retain
so much information.

Youthfront hosted a small gathering of about 50 youth workers from around North America to discuss a variety of books we'd been reading. I remember great conversations surrounding Andrew Root's *Revisiting Relational Youth Ministry: From a Strategy of Influence to a Theology of Incarnation* and Sarah Arthur's *The God-Hungry Imagination: The Art of Storytelling for Postmodern Youth Ministry*.

Brian McLaren was in Kansas City for his *Everything Must Change* tour, so we invited him to speak to our group. After about 40 minutes of Brian talking about missional youth ministry, new kinds of evangelism, and a variety of other themes, he opened it up for questions. A bunch of questions were asked, but one in particular grabbed my attention: "If you were a youth pastor, what would you want the students in your group to know? I mean, what would be the most important things you'd want to teach?" (By the way, Brian was a youth worker before founding Cedar Ridge Church.)

Brian responded by saying something like, "I'd want to teach on the Christological significances, the church as mission into the world, and God's undeniable grace and mercy." Brian continued, "But! I'd like to flip that question back to you and ask you this: What one thing are you going to help your students experience now and into the future in order that when life gets completely chaotic, they have the ability to remain in the faith? What one thing?"

The conversation between Brian and that youth worker has led me to think hard about that "one thing" or the simplest, yet most extensive God-truths revealed in the Bible that I'd want our students to know before they leave our reach. And I've concluded that my "one thing" is the kingdom of God as outlined and comprised by three parts:

1. The Missio Dei (the mission of God)

2. The Imago Dei (the image of God)

3. The Opus Dei (the work of God)

THE MISSION OF GOD (MISSIO DEI)

I began (and would encourage you to begin doing the same in your youth ministry) helping students understand the mission of God. I believe it's out of God's mission that the imago Dei and the opus Dei truly have context and meaning, thereby helping our students understand and engage in the missio Dei. The missio Dei informs the implication, integration, and application of God's Story for each of our lives. The interaction between the imago Dei and the opus Dei works to point back to our participation in God's activity, fulfilling God's mission.

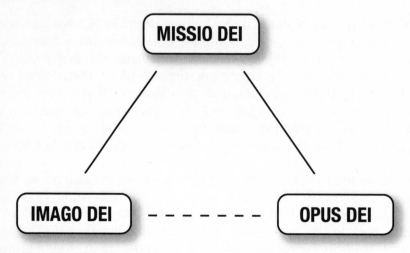

As I've already mentioned, the mission of God is—

- God the Father (Proclaim) sending the Son (Presence)

- God the Father and the Son sending the Spirit (Previence)

- God the Father, the Son, and the Spirit sending the church (Practice) into the world for the purpose of salvation and justice[47]

If we're going to inspire, challenge, and equip a generation of students to be about the mission of God, then we must help them discover the characteristics of the mission. It's out of the discovery of God's mission, the formation of a deep connection with it, followed by an even deeper commitment to it that students will engage in the missio Dei.

We've drawn several conclusions about God's mission in previous chapters. However, for the specific purpose of this chapter, I offer the following as 12 essential characteristics of God's mission that are revealed through God's Story and which our students just can't miss. They can't miss them as being essential, and they can't engage in God's mission without them.

1. God's mission is fully trinitarian. There's no question that the mission of God involves all of the Godhead. Without any one of the three Persons, the church (or more specifically, our youth ministries), which practices the kingdom work proclaimed by God and made present by Jesus and made able by the Holy Spirit, is left to splash around on its own and try to keep her head above water.

2. God's mission is overtly personal. God has called each and every one of us to be a part of his mission. No one is able to test out or opt out of it. God's mission is both private and public. It's private because it influences our own spiritual growth and discovery; it's public because it's seen by the world. However private or public, it's personal. God's mission is directly related to each one of us, and it's out of each of our natures and uniquenesses that we carry the mission out into the world.

3. God's mission is explicitly communal. We're each called to be agents of God's restoration, but we don't operate alone. Rather, we function in what's intended to be a deeply united people, a community that's marked by its love, inclusiveness, and belonging—called the church.

4. God's mission is wonderfully holistic. God's mission isn't merely about saving souls. It's about the entirety of a person. This is why we'd define God's mission as having two goals or objectives: *Salvation* (the soul) and *justice* (which intends to touch others' social, physical, environmental, and economic needs, as much as their spiritual ones).

5. God's mission is thoughtfully political. By *political* I don't mean that God's mission has red states and blue states. I do, however, mean that God's mission is intended to reach into all areas of life, including public matters. The mission of God supersedes the common world and makes its way into the affairs of the state, which is why I believe we all should be politically aware and active.

6. God's mission is unequivocally ecumenical. I love the recent unity and partnership I've felt among my friends in other denominations and segments of Christendom. My Catholic friends in Kansas City and beyond are as interested in the mission of God as any of my evangelical Protestant friends are. The mission of God transcends the theological boundaries that so many of us keep in order to be "right."

7. God's mission is deliberately cooperative. Yes, by *cooperative* I mean that God's mission is a joint mission between God and his people and between the divergent people of God. I also mean that God's mission isn't just about the church or those who serve in the church. Since God's activity is all around us and we enter into what God is already doing, God's mission can also be found in the schools, in the workplace, in the university, and in the government.

8. God's mission is distinctly Christian. A Christian is one who believes in Jesus Christ and whose life is derived from Jesus' teachings. Therefore, in order for God's mission to be Christian, it must involve the life, voice, deeds, and teachings of Jesus. Oftentimes when we're dealing with the missio Dei, we can lose focus on the proper concept of Jesus. Jesus is the perfect image of God. Without it, we have no one to guide our lives or a way to guide the rest of the world to see God.

9. God's mission is intentionally contextual. The mission of God is best activated when it's pertaining to the context in which we minister. Each of our contexts looks and feels different, but God's mission carries with it a message from Jesus that's transportable into any and all contexts. One isn't more receptive than another.

10. God's mission is enduringly undividable. God's mission can't be separated into parts. In other words, God's mission isn't designed to reflect only certain characteristics of God or teach certain passages of Scripture. The mission of God is a take-all-or-nothing kind of mission. We can probably think of people who use only the parts they like best. If we're honest, we'll even admit to fighting the urge to divide the mission of God into the parts we believe to be the most important. And sure, there are times, depending on the context, when we'll emphasize certain aspects of God's narrative and mission over others. However, that shouldn't be a permanent practice.

11. God's mission is excitingly mysterious. We know God works in mysterious ways. We know the things of God are above us and his ways are higher than our ways. Embracing the mystery and wonder of God's mission helps us enthusiastically embrace the unplanned and unpredictable experiences in our youth ministries.

12. God's mission is increasingly expansive. One of the most telling aspects of the mission of God is its expansiveness. The mission of God is real and working. We know this is true because the church, God's agent of mission, is growing both numerically and spiritually. And as the church grows, the mission of God grows. At times you may not feel as though your particular faith community is growing numerically. However, think about the universal aspect of God's mission and be encouraged!

THE IMAGE OF GOD (IMAGO DEI)

Scripture isn't packed with verses or ideas to help us better understand what it means to have been created in God's image. But it's still a vital part of God's revelation and our understanding of his mission. We do know that the opening chapter of the beginning book in the narrative of God, Genesis, tells us that humans have been created in the "image of God":

> Then God said, "Let us make man in our image, after our likeness. And let them have dominion over the fish of the sea and over the birds of the heavens and over the livestock and over all the earth and over every creeping thing that creeps on the earth." So God created man in his own image, in the image of God he created him; male and female he created them. (Genesis 1:26-27, ESV)

To be created in God's image means to have been created with intellect, emotion, and will. It also means, however, that we're created to be a living representation of God, a symbol intended to show forth the glory of God. We need to help our students understand that they're symbols of God, created in his image.

There are a number of important things that students must know as it relates to being designed, broken, and reshaped into the image of God.

Designed in God's Image

Being created in the image of God has implications for our lives. Here is a short list of significant matters—revealed by Scripture—that are related to being created in God's image. Our students *must* know these things.

- *God is God and we are not.* We're to be a humble people who remember our position in creation. We're a created image because God is the ultimate reality.

- *Humans are valuable.* We're to remain aware of our value or our intrinsic worth. The fact that the ultimate reality, God, chose our image proves our value, as does the fact that God created us to have a relationship with him.

- *We represent, but we also reflect.* To represent is to stand for or to symbolize, but to reflect is so much more. To reflect is to show a mirror image of or to send something forth. In God's image we send forth the glory of God into the world.

- ***All of life, not just humans, is important.*** All of life is important. Plants, animals, fish, and so on all have a place in the kingdom of God. To be created in God's image is to be a caretaker over all of the earth.

- ***God alone is to be worshipped.*** God is the ultimate reality, and we're the created image of that reality. As that image we're considered by God to be "very good." Therefore, no other created being on earth or object fabricated by people is more worthy of our worship than God.

Broken Images of God

Because of the sin of Adam and Eve, we're naturally broken, cracked, marred, and smudged. We're no longer "very good" images of God. Rather, we're in need of repair; of restoration.

- ***Relationships are broken.*** The relationship we have with God and others is inherently broken. We're only able to reunite with God and live in community with others through the death and resurrection of Jesus.

- ***Pain and suffering are very real.*** Each of us, although created in God's image, will experience hurt, pain, and discomfort. Life is hard; therefore, anguish, distress, and affliction are all part of the journey of life.

- ***Death is temporary for those who believe.*** There's no doubt that death is real. However, for those of us who believe in Jesus, death is only temporary. Death is a result of being broken and separated from God. But through God's gift of salvation and justice—Jesus—we have victory over death. *Christus Victor!*

- ***The garden of Eden was a real place, and one day it will be whole again.*** The garden will be a whole environment again— metaphorically or otherwise. God will take up residence with us once more, and all things will be made new. We will one day experience the wholeness, peace, and beauty of the garden, as we remain faithful to God for all of eternity.

Reshaped Images of God

There is within each of us a desire to conform to the Person and work of Jesus Christ. Jesus, our model for life and ministry, has put his life on display that it might be followed or imitated. Jesus has also left the Holy Spirit for us. Through his ministry the Holy Spirit guides us and shapes us into newly designed images of God.

- **Jesus is the perfect image of God.** As sons and daughters of God, following after the Son of God, we're able to see and realize a life in the way of Jesus. Becoming like Jesus and expressing his values, we shine forth the glory of God.

- **Jesus is the hope.** It's in Jesus that we see the hope—not only the hope of the world, but also the hope of dwelling with God again as the garden curse will be snapped and God's creation will be restored. It's in Jesus that we see the wholeness that God has prepared (again) for us.

- **Jesus is the cause of life.** In the perfect image of Jesus, we see a harmonious relationship with God the Father. We also see the mission of God in which we're to be consistently active.

The image of God is essential. We must provide a clear and concise understanding of what it means to be created in the image of God for our students. Too many of them cannot even think about—and therefore cannot articulate—what it means to live in the image of God. This is obviously a problem if we truly believe that the rising generations can change the world through God's work.

THE WORK OF GOD (OPUS DEI)

The final element of God's kingdom is the work of God or the opus Dei. The work of God is simply the church's (or in our case, youth ministry's) involvement with the mission of God. The mission of God helps students see the personality of God and his desires for this broken world. The image of God helps students see themselves as they've been created and as they currently exist. And the work of God outlines for us the particular practices that employ the mission of God.

When I've presented the content of this book to a live audience, there's been a time or two when questions have arisen about the difference between God's mission and God's work. So in case you're wondering the same thing, let me take a moment to distinguish between the two.

First, mission isn't a chief activity of the church, but rather an attribute of God. In fact, most scholars place the mission of God inside the doctrine of the Trinity, not inside the doctrine of the church or salvation. Therefore, the church (or youth ministry) shouldn't believe that its task is the missio Dei. Instead, the church and its segments are *participants* in the missio Dei. Mission is what God is doing to restore the world through God's work, the gathering of people (called the church) who are reorienting their lives to celebrate the mission.

Second, the work of God is what God is doing through the church and our youth ministries to galvanize and complete the missio Dei. To participate in the mission is to participate in the movement of God's love toward people, since God is a fountain of sending love.[48] The church and its youth ministries must see their role inside the larger mission of God.

I believe it's imperative that our students understand the missio Dei, the imago Dei, *and* the opus Dei. If we're truly going to equip the rising generations to be about the things of God, then we must find creative ways to empower our students to develop a passion to be a lifelong part of the church. We'll look at more detailed descriptions of the following and other traits of narrative-missional work in youth ministry in chapter 8.

But for now, if I were backed into a corner and had to come out swinging with a description of the work of God, I'd say the work of God, and therefore the work of our youth ministries, is indisputably about—

- **Justice** There's no question that God wants the work of the church to be about justice. We're repeatedly called to make what is wrong in the world right. Justice is standing for fairness and equality; it's a commitment to provide dignity to, serve, and honor all people.

- **Transformation** This is different from change. Change just happens; it's inevitable. Transformation is what we hope for, what we pray for, and what we expect the Holy Spirit will do in the lives of our students and in the life of our community. When we carry out God's mission, we're transformed and so are our students. It isn't enough for youth ministries to simply open their doors and admit a new student or two, only to close the doors again and remain unaffected and untransformed except for the addition of a few names in the student ministry database.[49]

- **Relationships** Clearly, God is a relational God. To carry out the work of God means to find deeper union with God (more on this in chapter 7) and also deeper community with one another. Relationships are central to justice, which is filled with not only acts of compassion and kindness, but also restoration—restoring relationships with the poor and vulnerable and restoring them into a new community.

- **The Holy Spirit** The work of God is directly connected to the work of the Holy Spirit. It's by the Spirit that Jesus is born, anointed at his baptism, and led into the desert. It's in the power of the Holy Spirit that Jesus enters into his earthly ministry of teaching and healing.[50] It's through the Holy Spirit's previousness that the disciples are used to usher in Pentecost.[51] Youth ministries that are committed to the opus Dei are committed to being led by the Holy Spirit. After all, it's in the power of the Holy Spirit that the universal work of salvation is brought into this world today, convicting the world and expanding the fullness of the truths of God that have yet to be grasped.[52]

- **Love** It seems obvious, but the work of God has its origin in God's love for all of creation. The mission of God, and therefore the work of our youth ministries, is a movement of God's love toward people, since God is a fountain of sending love.[53] It's out of our commitment to love one another that our youth ministries will truly be places of belonging—places of refuge and retreat.

- **The kingdom of God** The term "kingdom of God" is admittedly rare in the Old Testament, but it's present. And the kingdom of God is at the very center of Jesus' teaching. The kingdom, as Jesus taught, is God's sovereign reign over humanity and humanity's willingness to submit to God's reign. In perhaps its most succinct definition, the kingdom of God is both the appearance and awareness of God's plan of salvation in all of its beauty and abundance. Youth ministries that are about the work of God are kingdom-focused communities seeking to find ways to bring salvation and justice to the whole world.

• **Conversion** Kingdom-focused youth ministries must be about evangelism or sharing the good news as preached by Jesus. And evangelism leads to conversion—the kind that restores the soul to God and restores the entire person into community (which is also being converted from old to new). Conversion isn't simply about "making converts." It's about converts altering their lives, repenting from the old way to live in a new way, and doing it all within community.

• **Holiness** The work of God, in as much it performs God's mission, is also about a holy people. And they're holy in two fashions. First, the work of God (his people who make up the church), are set apart as a community to be a royal priesthood. They are to be a representation of Jesus that brings light to a darkened world.[54] Second, the people of the church are to be about personal holiness. God's work is made eminent when the people choose to become people who are devoutly sacred and trying to live their lives in alignment with the intended ways of God.

The work of our youth ministries is to do the work of God. Each of our youth ministries will carry out God's mission through our work in distinctly different ways. Because of our varying contexts, leadership styles, and passions, our youth ministries won't look exactly like any other—and I think that's terrific. The greater the range of diversity in our ministries, the more I believe it represents God's mission—a beautiful mosaic colored vividly with its love, mercy, and grace—and provides for the spiritual and physical well-being of humanity.

The Story of God provides revelation. We understand God better when we understand how God is revealed through three things, (1) the mission of God in which we're called to impart our own being, (2) the image of God in which we're created, and (3) the work of God in which we're to commit our lives. Those three essential aspects of God's revelation are imperative for our students to understand, as they might also begin to inform their theology. And an informed theology provides a theological foundation that makes way for our students to take ideas and concepts about God from primarily being an intellectual exercise to making them a practical reality.

Reflection and Discussion Questions

*Chapter 4—Revelation: God's Story as the Context for Our Participation
in God's Mission*

- How is God revealing himself today through special revelation?

- In your opinion, how is revelation best understood? Is it through experience, culture, proposition, Scripture, or all of the above?

- What factors contribute to the conceptual noise in your students' minds?

- How might youth workers be to blame for the conceptual noise?

- What items are essential to you, personally, for helping students understand what it means to know and experience God?

- In what ways can you be more effective in your pursuit to help students see what it means to be created in God's image?

- How might God's mission be thoughtfully political?

- What are some of the mysterious ways you've seen God work out his mission?

- What are some of the areas in your life in which God is making you more holy?

CHAPTER 5

Foundation: God's Story as the Context for Our Theology

Youth ministry is about ecosystems. Therefore, that makes you and me conservationists. As youth workers, we have the privilege to care for a natural community comprised of at least two of the basic elements of every ecosystem: Environments and living organisms. As conservationists, then, we're primarily responsible for the interaction or the correlation between the environment and the living organisms.

As people committed to today's youth, we all work very hard to create transformational youth ministries. We're consistently working to create healthy environments (think programs or other opportunities to connect with students). We're also consistently working to engage students relationally. That, in a nutshell, is what youth ministry is about. Transformational youth ministry is increasingly concerned with the environments we create and the relationships we initiate, develop, and sustain.

Our job, therefore, is not just to care for environments and living organisms separately, but to oversee the interaction between those two things. As you'll see in the illustration below, youth workers ought to be (and, for the most part, I believe they are) deeply concerned with the overlap or the coming together, the interaction between the programs (environments) and the students and families (living organisms).

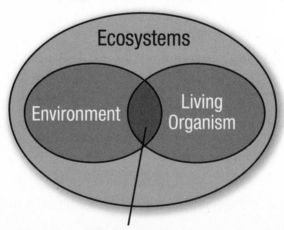

Interaction: The youth worker as conservationist

TRANSFORMATIONAL YOUTH MINISTRY

A few years ago, I was asked to define transformational youth ministry for an article in a magazine. Here's what I came up with:

> At its core, transformational youth ministry is the ongoing, holistic process of guiding students toward becoming like Jesus. It is a process of shepherding students through a journey of the spiritual life that fundamentally begins with a shepherd-student relationship, progresses with and through shared spiritual discovery and growth, and ends only when the shepherd-student relationship ceases to remain.[55]

In cooperation with other influences, such as parents, it's the youth ministry's aspiration, responsibility, and function to help provide for the transformative spiritual discovery, growth, and development of our students' faith. And we see God open the door to that transformative growth and development when we create imaginative and life-changing interactions between the programs we facilitate and the students we have relationships with.

Attentive youth workers seek to make sure the interactions they oversee are about the following foundational aspects of transformational youth ministry:

- *Ongoing* Transformational youth ministry evolves without interruption—meaning, youth workers realize the interaction between the environment where students live and the students themselves never stops. And in that realization, they seek to find ways to keep the movement toward growth and development going.

- *Holistic* Transformational youth ministry, like the mission of God, is concerned with the whole person—the soul, yes, but also the intellectual, physical, emotional, and social aspects of a student's life.

- *Process* Transformational youth ministry realizes that the interaction between the programs and the students is about process, not a product. This is often talked about in youth ministry; but I still see too many youth workers seeking accomplished outcomes in the lives of students, rather than in the *learning process* of students. Is youth ministry about the fulfillment of certain aspects of godliness or helping students realize the necessary aspects of a life with God that make godliness attainable?

- *Guiding* Obviously connected to the importance of transformational youth ministry being a process, guiding our students involves dealing with unfinished people, not completed projects.

- *Jesus* It seems obvious, but transformational youth ministry that's contextualized within the mission of God and the work of God is all about living and loving in the way of Jesus.

Creating interactions and giving guidance as a conservationist within the interactions initiated and sustained by the Holy Spirit is simply about helping students develop a practical theology. Practical theology moves theology from an intellectual exercise to a practical reality by taking the ideas and concepts of God and making them true in the world. Transformational youth ministry guides what is in the mind and moves it first into the heart and ultimately into the physicality of our students. We use our hands, feet, eyes, ears, and so on when we live out the ideas of God and make theology tangible.

It's no doubt a very difficult task of youth ministry, but somehow we have to find methods for transformational youth ministry that inspire, equip, and challenge students to become students of practical theology. Conservationists are keenly alert to the foundational aspects of the ecosystem that make it transformational, such as its ongoing, holistic, process-oriented, guiding, and Jesus-centered nature. Conservationists should also be alert to the essential traits of transformational youth ministry. For it's within and outside of the following traits that we cultivate and sustain (with the guidance of the Holy Spirit) transformative interactions with the students in our youth ministries.

Youth ministry that's transformational is—

- Built on a platform of unconditional love

- Patient and forgiving, realizing that transformation takes time

- Expectant of the work of the Holy Spirit

- Authentic and highly transparent

- Highly relational, engaging the entire family

- Creative and imaginative, chaotic and messy

- Dependent on prayer

- Encouraging and empowering

- Designed for the learner over the teacher

- Missionally minded (missio Dei)

- Committed to the entire narrative of God

- Fruitful and lasting

- Connected to the whole of the local and global church

APPLIED THEOLOGY

Out of the revelation of God, our theology is informed, and we build a foundation for a life of learning and growing with God. That foundation allows us to construct a life lived in the intended ways of God. Theology itself is ineffective when discovered outside of the narrative of God, and theology cannot be left discoverable without a method for helping students take the ideas of God and make them practical realities in their lives.

I believe many of us have a passion to help students develop a working theology. However, oftentimes our desire is far greater than our effectiveness. Few youth workers have an intentional process that truly provides a way for students to grasp and then live out the ideas of God. We shake our heads and wonder what we're doing wrong as we watch students graduate year after year without the ability to understand the things of God and how to make them tangible—to themselves and to the world.

I'd like to offer a process that might enable you to be more intentional and effective in helping your students construct a life in the intended ways of God based entirely on the revelation of God as seen through his grand narrative. This method is designed to assist you as you help students make the most of the interactions between their environment and their physical bodies.

I call this approach *applied theology*.[56] I certainly don't lay claim to the term *applied theology*. It's an old term that's been used in seminary classes and theology textbooks all over the world. However, I choose to use the term for the purpose of articulating a model for learning theology.

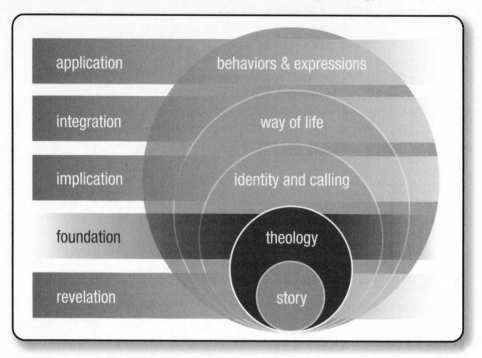

I use this term not only for its straightforwardness, but also for its meaning. Something that's applied has had the ability to be performed. It implies there's already been some kind of action or learned behavior affiliated with it. Applied theology is a method that gives youth workers the ability to best care for the interaction between the environments (programs) and the living organisms (students) in the ecosystem they inhabit.

FIVE ASPECTS OF APPLIED THEOLOGY

This method of applied theology has five essential aspects that operate as one unit in complete conversation and interdependence.

These aspects are (1) interaction, (2) intersection, (3) interchange, (4) identification, and (5) immersion. Sure, one or more of these aspects can be performed exclusive of the others. I contend, however, that if any aspect is disconnected from the others, it won't provide for the ongoing function of the whole. I believe this is largely where youth workers find themselves at a loss today—implementing only certain aspects and doing so outside of the reality of the whole.

The five aspects of applied theology are very fluid. In other words, in their interconnectedness there still exists a measure of changeability or pliability. They're more blurry than clear. For example, when a student might move from one aspect to another is largely dependent on the individual, not on the interaction itself. We can't make students grow; we can only help guide them as they grow.

It's also important to note that I believe students can enter into the process of these aspects of applied theology at various points. As we move on to define each of these segments in the following paragraphs, remember that some students may enter into the process during the Interchange or even during the experience of an Immersion.

In summary, the five aspects are interconnected to one another, fluid, and accessible at various points depending on the condition of the environment and the composition of the student.

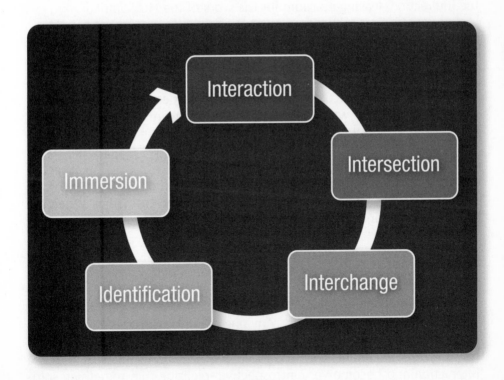

Interaction

This is the matter or the content that brings the environmental attributes and the personal characteristics of the student inside the ecosystem together. There's no need to manufacture the specific elements of the Interaction. The Interaction between the programming (various environments) and the student will turn up specific elements of the organic Interaction.

The Interaction might be a weekly program such as a Sunday school class, a seasonal retreat, a trip to the soup kitchen, or a one-on-one setting over coffee. Regardless, the natural experience resulting from the environment we create and the student that God has created is one of the five integral aspects of applied theology.

Many youth workers don't trust the environment they've created, and they're tempted to manufacture what the student might learn from the Interaction. Many youth workers are afraid of their students' imaginations—that the creative thinking from within the mind and heart of a student will result in not fully grasping the truths of God as they themselves believe. As a result, many youth workers (sometimes even unintentionally) manipulate the Interaction, leaving no room for the work of the Holy Spirit.

Intersection

This is where the Interaction experienced and the personal story of the student collide. In some way, the student becomes aware of how his personal narrative intersects with the Interaction. At this point in the applied learning cycle, the student has an experience in which he sees how he might very well share a similar story with someone else. The Interaction aspect of the applied theology cycle can be merely a moment of observation. However, at the Intersection stage in this cycle, there's no spectating. When the theology of God intersects with a student's life, it becomes deeply personal very quickly.

Perhaps you've noticed the change in a student's behavior when theology gets deeply personal. Some common responses are to quit, to turn around in fear and run like the wind, or to become paralyzed by fear (either temporarily or for an extended time). Any one of these responses makes it very difficult for the student to process the private intrusion (intersection) into his story. Other students will recognize how their stories intersect with the Interaction and become very introspective, realizing that something spiritual or theological is happening within them.

I vividly remember taking a small group of students to a homeless shelter in Chicago. And I mostly remember it because of one student's reaction to the Interaction. As we were leaving the shelter to go home, this student whispered to me, "I see myself in that building. I see myself in each of those people. I see myself in the pain of those people." That kind of experience is a theological intrusion or a point of Intersection between the experience and the individual story of the student. At this point, God has punctured the soul, and the student has felt it, recognized it, and has been drawn more into God because of it.

I want to emphasize the importance of guiding the students within your ecosystem to make observations and to deeply reflect on the Interaction and the intrusion at this stage of the applied theology cycle. Probably one of the best ways to do that is through the process of reflective journaling. Reflective journaling is important because it makes connections between the new experience of the Interaction and their previous knowledge.[57] When students intentionally take a moment to write down what they're learning, the connections between the Interaction and the resulting new discoveries are reinforced and expanded.

Below are some thoughts on the importance of reflective journaling from Terry Doyle, author of *Helping Students Learn in a Learner-Centered Environment*.

> Reflective journaling greatly enhances students' understanding and recall because the very fact of writing causes them to move their ideas from the abstract world inside their brains into the concrete world outside their brains. Writing causes them to translate this new learning into their own words and produce it in a clear and organized manner, which will only be possible if they understand what they've learned.[58]

The simple activity of transferring the learning from the mind to the heart to the hand to the paper is the first action toward the practice of the final stage of the applied theology cycle, Immersion. As you create the space and time for reflective journaling, consider asking guided questions to help your students more fully connect the Interaction to their feelings caused by the intrusion experience.

When done in a meaningful way, the reflective journaling experience can:

- Help maximize the possibility for students to connect the new experience with previous experiences

- Help students make emotional connections to the experience, increasing the potential for remembering the now multiple stories outside of the Interaction

- Help students move from merely gathering new "data" from the Interaction to being able to produce future knowledge

- Help expand the students' views of the world by allowing them to record from their own experiences the possible observations that others might make from the same Interaction

- Help expand the number of cues the students can respond to in order to recall the experience, allowing them to interact with the things of God in deeper, more robust ways[59]

Interchange

In addition to the importance of reflective journaling, I also can't stress enough the importance of the opportunities that you and I have to dialogue with our students. Coming out of a moment of theological Intersection or intrusion comes the significant—and I believe in many ways primary—activity of conversation. Students need a place to process all that they're learning and experiencing.

Because of its incredible importance, the opportunities of exchanging ideas, thoughts, and questions can't be treated with flippancy or an under appreciation for the opportunity itself. Conversation with students is unbelievably momentous. I believe we sometimes move past the conversation too quickly or control the conversation, not allowing students to really process their thoughts. Instead, we need to shut up and let students do the talking. (It's blunt but true.) That doesn't mean we sit thoughtlessly in silence. But it does mean we regulate our desire to talk and be wise with our own words.

At this point in the oversight of the applied theology cycle, youth workers are better off asking guiding questions than making assertions. We're more helpful when we create dialogue to help students arrive at the critical matters of faith, rather than simplistically trying to push students where they don't want to go or where they might not be ready to go.

When leading healthy, effective environments of dialogue, it's important to remember the following.

- **Lay down some ground rules.** For example, no interrupting, and so on.

- **Refrain from dominating the conversation.** You're there to facilitate others' learning, not push your own ideas.

- **Show interest through your body language and facial expressions.** If you aren't interested or show you're bored in some way, then the students in your group will also be bored.

- **Ask open-ended questions.** Avoid asking yes-or-no questions.

- **Communicate clearly.** Try hard not to mix metaphors as it can cause confusion.

- **Manage the feelings of the students in conversation.** Allow for periods of silence if a student is sad, angry, confused, happy, disappointed, and so on.

- **Encourage humor, but with respect.** Avoid using sarcasm, as it isn't always considered humor (especially by those receiving the sarcastic remarks).

- **Be prepared while remaining flexible.** You may talk about only one general theme or one specific experience during your time in the dialogue. And that's okay. (Think conceptual noise.)

- **Be aware of the time but not driven by it.** While you will always have time constraints, do your best to allow the discussion to develop naturally. Don't be afraid of silence, as it gives students a chance to process their thoughts.

- **Realize the importance of being a co-learner.** You should present yourself during these times of dialogue not as the expert, but as a learner on the same plane as the students.

- **Be patient and realize that God is at work.** The Holy Spirit has work to do in drawing students to God—don't get in the way of it.

- **Be respectful of various opinions.** Your opinion, idea, or experience as a co-learner is definitely appropriate. But as the facilitator, you must remember that everyone else's opinions, ideas, and experiences are appropriate as well.

- *Keep the conversation going.* Ask questions that are specific to the experience, to the student's current place of discovery, and to the future formation that may come out of the learnings.

Identification

At this point in the cycle of applied theology, students have already participated in a transformative Interaction and discovered how their own individual story is Intersected by the Interaction and the specific experiences and details of it. As a result of the Intersection, students have been given the appropriate opportunity for reflective journaling and an exchange of ideas, thoughts, and questions through the Interchange aspect. So it's at this stage that students begin compiling the observations they've made, the reflections they've considered, the conversations they've shared, and the questions they've pondered, and they start grappling with the mystification of what it means specifically for their own lives.

Identification is when a student begins not only to accept what the narrative of God, through a specific Interaction, means for her life, but also begins to lay claim to its importance in her own life. Progressively, the student begins to connect the dots. She begins to find ways to match up the array of feelings, thoughts, and statements she's shared and finds herself slowly—or sometimes quickly—owning the experienced truth she's come to apprehend and appreciate.

I'm reminded of a student in one of the youth ministries I served—we'll call him Rick. Rick was the son of two rather well-known and involved people in the church. He was a good student in school, and he was well-behaved at our youth gatherings. Occasionally, Rick would show signs of a deep interest in the things of God. But mostly, he just went about youth group doing his thing. He was friends with nearly everyone, and he pitched in to help set up and tear down the sound equipment, load the vans on a retreat, and do whatever else he could to help.

Even though Rick was a regular part of all of our programs and an active participant in small-group discussions, it wasn't until Rick was placed into a situation with a homeless person that he really began to take ownership of and profoundly identify with his own faith. During a trip to a student conference where I was speaking, Rick was walking down the street when he noticed a homeless person leaning against the wall near a pay phone. We were walking to a local sandwich shop at the time, and all the while we were saying how hungry we were. However, as Rick would tell it, when he saw the homeless person and the sign for the sandwich shop together in one glance, he was no longer as hungry as he'd been. This wasn't the first homeless person Rick had ever seen; but for some reason, the compilation of all that he'd been learning through the years, the development and growth in his own life, and the new way that Rick was beginning to see the world led him to use the remaining cash in his pocket to buy the homeless person a giant sandwich.

I could see on Rick's face—for the first time ever—that somehow the divine combination of all that he'd come to learn through Scripture, tradition, experience, and reason finally meant something for him. He finally knew what it meant to bring justice to a broken world. He finally knew what it meant to view the world through eyes of compassion and not comparison. That day Rick identified with his faith and his theology in way he'd never done before.

Several weeks later, Rick initiated our church's first ministry to homeless people. Today, the ministry still flourishes as literally hundreds of students have passed out sandwiches, hygiene products, ponchos, and a variety of other helpful items to thousands of homeless people.

These are the kinds of things that begin to happen when students identify with their faith, theology, and the mission of God. I'm sure you have your own stories of similar things that have occurred in your youth ministry. Don't underestimate the work you've done as a conservationist to allow for the interaction between the environments and the living organisms in the ecosystem you care for.

Immersion

At this place in the cycle, students begin retelling the narrative of God in their own way as they live out practical theology. What was once an intellectual exercise has become an applied reality.

At this stage students have determined to pour themselves into the environment in which they reside. They're no longer searching for a reason, context, or meaning—they're only searching for ways they might instill the culture with the things of God, and the things of God with culture.

This retelling of the narrative isn't a narrative the students have conjured up on their own. Rather, it's the narrative of God as understood through the Intersection of God's narrative with their own personal narratives. This is what we all dream about, hope for, and pray for—transformation!

Beginning with the Interaction and then moving on to the Intersection, Interchange, and Identification, the Immersion experiences are intermittent for sure. However, they're no longer discontinuous opportunities designed by youth workers who are "supposed" to do that. Instead, they're events that we've had nothing to do with—other than years of commitment to the work of God.

The Immersion aspect of this applied theology cycle might be intermittent, but it isn't temporary. Each Immersion experience is in fact a new Interaction, thus the establishment of a virtuous cycle that leads to continual shared spiritual growth and discovery—that lasts a lifetime.

Spiritual Formation for the Mission of God

Transformational youth ministry is about an ongoing, holistic process of guiding students toward becoming like Jesus. Therefore, it's about helping students build a foundation for continued spiritual growth and discovery that continues to deepen their theological considerations and commitments, while at the same time it informs the identity and calling for their lives, thereby shaping them into people who are living out the mission of God.

I think it's essential to understand that your students will enter this cycle at various points and different levels of interest. Students will determine where they want to jump in and experience God. Some will be more apt to engage the Interaction stage and others will be drawn to the Immersion stage. It's important to remember, as the conservationist, that there are many environmental conditions which will engage your students. Lean into the ministry of the Holy Spirit as you help establish a transformational youth ministry.

Reflection and Discussion Questions
Chapter 5—Foundation: God's Story as the Context for Our Theology

• How would you define transformational youth ministry?

• If youth workers are truly conservationists, as chapter 5 suggests, then what is our biggest task(s)?

• Take a moment to reflect on the list of traits of transformational youth ministry on pages 82-83. What might be missing from this list? Which trait(s) stands out to you the most?

• On a scale of 1 to 10, with 10 being the most, how well do you do trust the Holy Spirit in your ministry events and programs? What keeps you from trusting more deeply?

• What personal stories can you share that would illustrate the behaviors you've noticed in students when their souls have been intersected with the things of God?

• How might you guide students in the reflective journaling process more effectively?

• When you facilitate group dialogue, what do you consider to be your strengths? What do you consider to be your growth areas?

• What would you consider to be signs that reveal your students are beginning to identify with the things of God in deep, meaningful ways?

• What would you say are the key components of an Immersion experience?

PART TWO: SIGNS

Patty Griffin is one of my favorite singer-songwriters. Her beautiful voice coupled with her imaginative storytelling and her compelling passion is deeply moving. When I listen to her music, I'm reminded of a God who creates with such precision and care. *How could anything so beautiful be from anywhere other than God?* I ask myself as I get lost in the music and lyrics.

Among many of Griffin's brilliant works is a song entitled "When It Don't Come Easy." It's a rich song about challenge, love, change, wondering, and companionship. Griffin sings,

> ...I don't know nothing except change will come
> Year after year what we do is undone
> Time keeps moving from a crawl to a run
> I wonder if we're gonna ever get home
>
> You're out there walking down a highway
> And all of the signs got blown away
> Sometimes you wonder if you're walking in the wrong direction
>
> But if you break down
> I'll drive out and find you
> If you forget my love
> I'll try to remind you
> And stay by you when it don't come easy...[60]

Do you ever feel as though everything you do is undone? Do you ever feel like you're wandering down a highway while wondering about your purpose and it seems as though all of the signs were blown away? Do you ever feel as though you're walking in the wrong direction? I do. I often find myself wandering and wondering, *Am I in the right place? Is this ministry to these kids really making that much of a difference? Are you even there listen-*

ing, God? Where are the signs that what I'm doing is working, helping, or even worth it?

If we're honest, we've all felt that way at some point in our lives. We've all been looking for a sign that points us in the right direction. We've all experienced that feeling of loneliness and being lost, wondering if we're doing the right things to make the right amount of impact in the lives of the students and families we minister to. Those feelings, of course, are natural; but they aren't fun.

It's a good thing that when it comes to what we're to be about in this world, God's signs are pretty clear. It may not always seem that way as we search for meaning and purpose in life. But the signs are there. Through the truths of the Bible, we have clear indications from God through gestures, presence, and symbols that we're to be about helping God restore his world. We're agents of God's restorative plan to bring the world toward its intended wholeness. The signs are pretty apparent.

Very simply, the signs for who we're to be and what we're to be about in this world are condensed ever so intentionally out of God's great narrative and into our identity, calling, and way of life. God is very unambiguous in his Word, and in the life and ministry of Jesus, that what we're to be about in God's image is his mission through his work.

Part two is designed to help you help your students understand their identity and calling and what it means to live a Jesus-centered lifestyle. Of course we desire for our students to live Jesus-centered lives because it's in Jesus that we see the personality, characteristics, and love of God demonstrated in tangible ways. If we desire for the world to embrace God, then we must be the physical presence of Jesus. The next two chapters provide a framework that will aid you in inspiring, challenging, and equipping your students with the understanding of their roles as agents of God's love and blessing.

God gives us signs. These signs aren't unlike the signs we see alongside the highway or in the midst of the city or even along the hiking trail. These signs point us in the right direction; give notice to the right path to take; and inform us of the points of oasis and rest, what to look for, and what to look out for. These signs are intended to be symbols for a way of life that helps us know how to more fully cooperate with God's mission.

CHAPTER 6

Implication: God's Story as the Context for Our Identity and Calling

The revelation of God as seen through the entire narrative informs our theological foundation, which provides the ability to understand our identity and calling.

Our identity is simply *who we are*. It's our uniqueness, personality, and characteristics that make us who we are and who we're becoming. Our calling is *what we've been created to do* or what our lives are to be about.

I don't know any students (or adults, for that matter) who don't wonder about their identity and calling. The question "Who am I?" comes up early in adolescence, and it arises out of the same maturation process that changes the physical appearance of our bodies, the composition of our inner lives, and our interactions with those around us. Typically, as students seek to find their identities, they'll frequently compare themselves to others or to the "ideal person" in their minds.

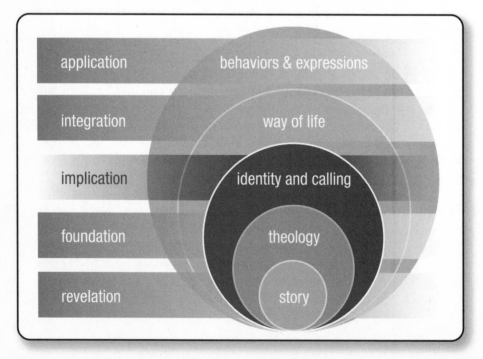

Part of our role as youth workers is to guide our students into the process of discovering who they are and what they're to be about. We must take seriously the importance of helping our students understand how they're caught up or implicated in the Story of God. It's in our identity and calling that we're both *characters* in and *contributors* to the Story.

IDENTITY: WHO AM I?

Identity Formation and Spiritual Formation

We've been created in the image of God with common overarching qualities that we share with all of humanity: A soul, the freedom to make decisions, wisdom for life, the ability to learn and gain knowledge, an innate awareness to love and be compassionate inside the realm of relationship (with God and others), and the ability to comprehend morality. These are all part of our shared identity as humans.

As youth workers, it's imperative that we understand how the students within our influence go about grasping their individual identities. It's in this identity formation that students will know how to best serve their communities.

I haven't found a better way to articulate this process of identity formation than through the writing of David Elkind, a specialist in adolescent psychology and a prolific author. In his standout book entitled *All Grown Up and No Place to Go*, Elkind provides the view that there are traditionally two ways that adolescents construct their identities.

First, there is the process of differentiation and integration, which is about separating out concepts, feelings, and emotions in order to put the parts together into a higher-ordered whole.[61] Typically, adolescents who form their identities in this way possess a strong sense of self and are able to direct their inner thoughts and feelings in ways that help them develop. They're also generally future-oriented. This means they're able to postpone the desired feelings of gratification, which allows them to be more comfortable with who they are and who they're becoming without the self-induced pressure to become someone they're not.

Second, juxtaposed to this concept of differentiation and integration is the concept of what Elkind calls substitution. Substitution is a process of replacing sets of concepts, feelings, and emotions for the purpose of forming an identity that isn't genuine to who the student really is. This process is also referred to as "the patchwork self," and it's characterized by picking and choosing the traits of one's peers and replacing the true self with the "self" of others.[62] According to Elkind, students who form their identities with a "patchwork" mentality are others-centered and directed, are very much about the present tense, and are less able to postpone feelings of gratification in order to feel good immediately.

It's imperative that youth workers realize that there's another natural process going on during teenagers' spiritual formation—they're also forming as human beings. This ought to shed a little light on why students are interested in spiritual things one moment, and then just one moment later they act as though they couldn't care less about spiritual matters. It may also help us to understand why time and patience are two very important keys to allowing students to form—both as human beings and as Christians.

This understanding of identity formation should also provide a more rational way of dealing with students who are troublesome at times or who do crazy things. Students do crazy things because they're thinking crazy thoughts. Remember this! Knowing this truth should pump more grace into you than frustration or concern. We must allow the natural process of identity formation to work alongside the process of Christian formation because these two things are inseparable. Human development and Christian formation happen in parallel execution.

Some of our students will never choose to accept the gift of salvation. It breaks my heart to think this, but it's true. Some people never engage in a restorative relationship with God. You probably try not to think about this too often, but somewhere in the back of your mind and deep in your heart, this reality lurks. I bring it up for one simple reason, and it certainly isn't to take the wind out of your sails. Instead, I mean to encourage you.

If we understand how our students form their identities and we allow them some freedom in that process while we guide their maturation through mentoring and other means, then what if our best intentions aren't enough? I mean, what if all we did with some of our students was help them become good citizens—would that be okay? Does the missio Dei leave room for God to do God's work through people who are merely good citizens and not Christ-followers? I'd like to believe that the mission of God transcends our intentions and that all things do work together for the good of God and one another.

I'm not sure how you feel about the idea that your work may shape the lives of merely good citizens instead of godly ones. But for me, it's still a win. If after several decades all I did was make the world a better place by raising good citizens, then it wouldn't be enough—but it would be *something*, which is better than nothing. The ministry you have with *all of your students*—believer or not-yet-believer—unquestionably matters to God and God's mission.

The Five Factors

Along with our common human characteristics, each of us has been created with an array of personal characteristics that distinctly belong to us. These characteristics come out of our identity formation, and they reveal who we are and how we're different from those around us.

It's widely understood that there are five major domains of personality. Sometimes they're referred to as the "Five Factor Model," and each factor contains a variety of qualities that help define our being.[63] While these five factors are the work of scientific and social research, it's still helpful to recognize them and understand how they relate to the discovery of our own identities and those of our students. Discovering the personality traits of these five areas helps us to better manage and navigate our relationships, whether they're within the family, school, or workplace.

We cannot begin to understand people if we don't understand ourselves. And, frankly, we can't begin to fully understand God if we don't understand ourselves, either. We are God's creations; therefore, we see God reflected in each other's faces as well as when we look in the mirror every day.

The following is a list of the five factors of personality and a sampling of some of the characteristics that comprise each one.

1. Openness—appreciation for art, emotional, adventurous, imaginative, curious, and variety of experience

2. Conscientiousness—self-discipline, act out of duty, desire to achieve, and planned behavior as opposed to spontaneous

3. Extraversion—desire for the company of others, tendencies to seek various motivational helps, typically positive and very energetic

4. Agreeableness—acting considerate and cooperative with others, as opposed to skeptical and antagonistic

5. Neuroticism—emotional instability, a tendency to wear one's emotions on the sleeve, and emotions such as anger, anxiety, depression, and helplessness are easily triggered[64]

You could probably list the names of your students in one column and then match the names with the appropriate factors listed above. But would your students know how to describe themselves? Do they see their unique qualities? Are your students able to articulate who they are?

They may not be ready or even want to discover all of what makes them who they are—and that's okay. But at some point, our students need to receive the tools to help them define themselves accurately and realistically. Otherwise, they'll constantly compare themselves with those around them and with the ideal vision of the person they'd like to be.

I'm not necessarily suggesting you prepare a series of talks or Sunday school lessons on the five factors above. I am, on the other hand, suggesting that you do all you can to help your students come to grips with who God created them to be as unique people and celebrate their differences.

Three Categories For Our Identity with Christ

As important and insightful as those scientifically and socially based factors are, they aren't enough. Therefore, it's critical that we help our students understand who they are in relationship to Jesus. Those students who've chosen to live under the reign of God and confess Jesus as the King of their lives have a significant identity with Jesus. And over the years, I've found that one way to assist them in discovering this identity is by categorizing the truths into three categories: (1) Chosen, (2) Valued, and (3) Protected.

If we desire to reveal to our students how they're implicated in God's Story and also inspire, equip, and challenge them to actively participate in God's mission and work, then these teenagers must know they're *chosen*, and they are therefore:

- Children of God (John 1:12)

- Friends of Jesus (John 15:15)

- Justified (Romans 5:1)

- Invited to live in unity and communion with Jesus (1 Corinthians 6:17)

- To be members of the body of Christ (1 Corinthians 12)

- Redeemed (Colossians 1:13-14)

- Complete in Jesus (Colossians 2:9-10)

- Able to access God through Jesus (Hebrews 4:14-16)

Students must also realize they're *valued*. It's understood that followers of Jesus are highly valued because they're:

- Fruit bearers (John 15:8)

- God's temple (1 Corinthians 3:16)

- Ministers of reconciliation (2 Corinthians 5:16-21)*

- God's workmanship (Ephesians 2:10)

- Able to do all things through Jesus who provides strength (Philippians 4:13)

*This is also the basis for the calling of our lives.

Finally, we must help our students know how God has made provision for his people so they might effectively contribute to his mission and work. God has *protected* his people, and therefore they are:

- Free from condemnation (Romans 8:1-2)

- Assured that God is working in all things for their ultimate good (Romans 8:28)

- Anointed and sealed by God (2 Corinthians 1:21-22)

- Able to complete the good works that God has begun in them (Philippians 1:6)

- Citizens of heaven (Philippians 3:20)

Dependent Formation

It's also important to note that as the natural process of identity formation and Christian formation work together to produce people of God who are committed to the missio Dei, individuals may look dramatically different from one another.

I emphasize this because, quite frankly, I'm frustrated with the way we project onto students what we believe they're *supposed* to look like and become as Christ-followers—as if there's some singular, perfect description of a disciple. There's no such thing. True, there are traits of discipleship (the fruit of the Spirit, for example) that may serve as evidence of disciples' genuine relationships with God, love for themselves, love for others, and love for the surrounding world. But with all of our differences (think identity formation and personality traits), how can we claim that we'll produce one type of disciple out of students who look like this or that? We're fighting against the wind.

I believe we should celebrate our uniquenesses and realize that students, like adults, aren't "self-originating, self-sustaining, or self-explanatory."[65] By *self-originating* I mean that we were all created by God's choice and the decision of our parents.

By *self-sustaining* I mean that we need other people and nature. First, we need our mothers and their nutrients. Second, we need the products of nature—including oxygen, food, water, and so on—to sustain us. And finally, we need relationships. We desperately need the love of others, inspiration, and ongoing support and encouragement to continue.

By *self-explanatory* I mean there is no such thing as a "typical human being" or a "typical Christian." You won't find two people who are 100 percent the same, ever. You can't configure a list of "perfect Christian" traits and expect to reproduce all of those traits in all of the students all of the time. With that said, I don't believe a list of Christian traits is inherently bad if, *and only if*, it's used as a guideline for effectiveness or even to measure the growth of your students and the impact of your ministry. (I'll present a list of the virtues of Jesus in chapter 7 and a list of four key areas of formation in chapter 8.) But please don't use one to try to make your students into perfectly identical Christians before they graduate. Using a list in such a dogmatic and irresponsible way damages the efforts of us all.

So helping our students know who they are in terms of their identities, personalities, and as followers of Jesus (forming Christians) is critical to their ability to see how they're implicated in the Story of God. Of course, it's my contention that students cannot realize how they're caught up with God's Story unless they're first made aware of God through his revelation and then become more aware of God through the development of a theological foundation.

CALLING: WHAT AM I TO BE ABOUT?

Reconciliation and Restoration

There are two types of calling: General and specific. The general calling is the one for all Christians to be ministers of reconciliation. The specific calling is that particular place within God's narrative and mission in which God chooses to use us to carry out his mission and work.

All of us are called to be ministers of reconciliation. God is actively in the process of bringing the world toward its intended wholeness, and God is using you and me to do it. We're agents of restoration.[66] We're called to take God's promise to Abraham (to become both a blessed nation and a blessing to the nations; see Genesis 15) out into the world through our love and generosity.

I'm more deeply concerned with helping students see themselves as ministers of reconciliation than I am with guiding their future careers. Honestly, I don't spend a lot of time thinking about how Johnny and Suzy will spend their days working. I do, however, consider how Johnny and Suzy see themselves as ministers of reconciliation. Whether they end up as mechanics, computer scientists, teachers, doctors, or pastors isn't important to me. What is important, however, is that Johnny and Suzy realize that no matter what they end up doing for work, they're called to be agents of God's love and restoration.

Second Corinthians 5:17-21 says,

> Therefore, if anyone is in Christ, the new creation has come: The old has gone, the new is here! All this is from God, who reconciled us to himself through Christ and gave us the ministry of reconciliation: that God was reconciling the world to himself in Christ, not counting people's sins against them. *And he has committed to us the message of reconciliation. We are therefore Christ's ambassadors, as though God were making his appeal through us.* We implore you on Christ's behalf: Be reconciled to God. God made him who had no sin to be sin for us, so that in him we might become the righteousness of God. (*emphasis added*)

God is actively at work, and we're to be actively at work with him as ministers of reconciliation. To be a minister of reconciliation means to be about the mission and work of God in a broken world. Probably the biggest role we play is that of healers. An agent of restoration seeks to bring peace and healing into a broken world full of pain, misery, suffering, confusion, and isolation. We must help our students see themselves as restorers or healers who bring peace and healing to all those they come in contact with.

An agent of restoration seeks to find ways to heal the minds and hearts of people as Jesus did. If we study the healing miracles of Jesus, we find that each miracle does two things. First, it restores people to God spiritually; and second, it restores people to a community physically.

Each of Jesus' healing miracles is intended to bring people to God and bring people back into community with one another. Therefore, as healers we, too, must seek ways to do that—to restore people to God and to one another.

THREE ESSENTIAL QUESTIONS

In order to help our students realize how they're implicated in God's narrative, I believe there are three essential questions that we must help them answer.

1. Who is Jesus?

2. What is the gospel?

3. What is the church?

Helping our students understand who they are is very helpful to their being and growth, but it's not enough. It's imperative that we provide the answers to the three questions above. Without them, students can miss the basis of what it means to be a minister of reconciliation through their general and specific calling.

WHO IS JESUS?

I believe it's critical to help students see the *person* and the *work* of Jesus. When I refer to the person of Jesus, I'm speaking of his nature and qualities. When I refer to the work of Jesus, I'm speaking of both his role as the Messiah or the Christ and the role he plays in the restoration of all things as he advocates for humanity.

There's too much to know about Jesus for me to cover everything in this book. And quite honestly, I'm not qualified to dig very deep into the person and work of God's Son. So I'll leave the real deep diving for people such as Green, McKnight, and Marshall.[67] However, I believe there are some really important things that we can help our students discover without being scholars ourselves. Helping our students understand who Jesus is brings context and meaning to who they're intended to be and what they're intended to be about.

The Person of Jesus

I believe it's essential for us to help our students answer the question "Who is Jesus?" with the following concepts of Christology found within the *person* of Jesus.

First, Jesus yielded to the Holy Spirit. The mission, message, and means of Jesus were executed in the power and presence of the Holy Spirit. We see this in several ways: Through Jesus' baptism, through the Spirit's guidance in the desert experience of temptation, as well as in Jesus' statement that he was anointed by the Spirit and that it was in the Sprit's power that he was beginning his ministry (Luke 4:18). We even read later in Acts 10:38 that Jesus was doing ministry in the power of the Holy Spirit.

Second, Jesus came to embody the kingdom of God and make it present among the people of Israel. We see evidence of this in Jesus' life, voice, and actions. His life on earth revealed that he pointedly ignored the "rules" of the day when it came to doing the good he cared about so passionately. His voice was one of proclamation, and his central message was that the kingdom of God was at hand. The actions of Jesus—his miracles and mighty works—cannot be interpreted in any other way than as signs to introduce and indoctrinate the teaching of the kingdom of God.

Third, Jesus was a person of prayer. Although not as readily seen as his life, voice, and actions, prayer and solitude was a persistent part of the person of Jesus. We see this no more clearly than in Mark 1:35 when, after a night of mighty works, Jesus escapes to a solitary place to refresh through prayer and solitude.

Fourth, we see Jesus' person as one of suffering. Jesus reveals to us his lasting presence as a suffering servant. In fact, suffering wasn't merely an outcome of Jesus' commitment to his mission, message, and means; it was the very mode in which he emptied himself to be a humble presence among the people of God.

Finally, Jesus desired to restore a community of people to be about his mission, message, and means long after his departure from earth. We commonly refer to the twelve disciples when we speak of this community. However, we know it was probably much larger than just the Twelve. To illustrate my contention, I point you to Acts 1:20-26, which describes how the Eleven need to select a replacement for Judas—someone who's been a part of the community from the beginning (John's baptism) to the very end (ascension). They ultimately pick Matthias by drawing straws. (Something we could never get away with today, huh?) But what's interesting to me is that neither Justus nor Matthias are even mentioned in the Gospels. However, when the Twelve became Eleven, as prophesied, one man from the wider missional community of Jesus was good to go.

The Work of Jesus

I believe it's essential for students to recognize the work of Jesus—as Prophet, Priest, and King. Beyond those three things, all other learnings about the work of Jesus will follow suit.

✳ **Prophet:** A prophet is commonly understood as being one who speaks the Word of God to man. Jesus, therefore, functions as a prophet by revealing God to us through his life, voice, and actions.

Jesus was a master teacher, a rabbi—a prophet who was viewed by both his friends and enemies as one who teaches with authority. Jesus spent the majority of his ministry time teaching the crowds about the kingdom of God. He consistently called the crowds to be a new community, a newly restored Israel that was to be about the mission and work of God. Jesus' life was dedicated to deconstructing an old way of life and pointing people to a newly constructed life with God.

As well as being a master teacher, Jesus was a miracle worker. His deeds were mighty, and his actions were sometimes bewildering. Raising people from the dead, turning water into wine, feeding thousands of hungry people, and healing many crippled and sick people were all evidence of Jesus' desire to be about the people.

Although Israel had a history with prophets, they didn't have any experience with a prophet like Jesus. The other prophets throughout Israel's history were like Jesus in that they communicated the things of God to the people. However, they were very *unlike* Jesus in that they weren't the source of the revelation.

After Jesus' crucifixion, death, burial, resurrection, and ascension, he didn't stop being a prophet. In fact, Jesus' communication or revelation to us remains in the form of the ministry of the Holy Spirit. He also speaks through our lives, voices, and actions.

It's of the essence for our students to understand Jesus as prophet. They must find context and meaning in the life of Jesus in order to truly accept their roles in the mission and work of God.

✝ **Priest:** As a prophet, Jesus represents God to man. So it might be said that as a priest, Jesus represents man to God. Jesus is an advocate. He pleads with God for the cause of salvation for all of humanity.

Hebrews 2:17 talks of Jesus' "being made like his brothers and sisters in every way."[68] Jesus sympathizes with our weaknesses, our sufferings, and our temptations like no other priest does or ever could (Hebrews 4:15).[69] Jesus shares in our humanity; yet at the same time, he gives himself unto death in order that we might be atoned for. Jesus advocates for us by standing in place of each one of us to receive the punishment of death in order that we might live.

Jesus continues to advocate for us today. He resides in the heavenly temple of God as the completed sacrifice and silences the accusations of Satan. Jesus' ministry of intercession also manifests itself in his continued role in our becoming holy. And Jesus provides ongoing love, care, and prayer for us as we go about our daily lives.

King: Jesus quietly yet clearly made it known though his teachings, miracles, and other deeds that he indeed was Israel's King. Although ultimately Jesus' death was a part of God's divine and merciful mission to atone for humanity's sin, it was Jesus' assertion that he was King of the Jews which ultimately led the people to cry out to Pilate for his death. As Israel's King and our King, Jesus rules over all of creation with all God-given authority on heaven and earth (Matthew 28:18).[70] Jesus specifically governs and protects the church on earth and his kingdom in heaven. And, of course, he's also the King over the kingdom that resides in every believer (John 18:36-37).[71]

Jesus as King has supreme authority over all of our lives. The purpose of his reign or lordship is to have all of humanity's heart so that by following him, we might also bring peace and justice into the world. Jesus flipped the traditional role of a king on its head by making himself a servant to his Father and to all of humanity. Because Jesus our King was a servant, we can also serve others, thereby revealing the kingship of Jesus to a broken, confused, and misplaced world full of people who are seeking to be loved and shown the way.

Jesus is our King. He is the ruler that Israel has been looking forward to, and he is the ruler that the people of God need constantly. As the head of the church, Jesus is therefore worthy of all our worship and praise.

Imperative Discoveries of Jesus as Prophet, Priest, and King

For so many students, especially those who haven't been introduced to a full narrative view of God's Son, Jesus is simply an idea. Most like the idea of Jesus, enjoy hearing stories about Jesus, and love learning about his controversial yet compassionate ways. However, generally speaking, students have a hard time connecting with Jesus in a personal way—even though they might say that they've accepted Jesus into their hearts.

For the following reasons, it's imperative that students understand Jesus as Prophet, Priest, and King:

- Students struggle to identify with Jesus in their daily lives. Helping students understand that Jesus still speaks to us today (through the Holy Spirit) will help them engage with Jesus on a deeper level.

- Students often have difficulty comprehending the doctrine of the Trinity. Showing students that Jesus is the source of revelation as well as the one articulating it assists them in grasping the doctrine of the Trinity.

- To many students, Jesus is untouchable. It's challenging for students to see how their lives and the life and ministry of Jesus intersect. Helping students understand that Jesus really knows what we're going through helps them make contact with Jesus in material ways.

- Jesus serves as King. He doesn't just reign as Lord. Actually, he serves *as* he reigns as Lord and King. Students know that most kings don't serve others but are served themselves. Helping students see Jesus as a Servant King helps them absorb a spirit of serving.

Students struggle to understand that Jesus lives within them. When we can help students see the kingdom of God and the ways of the kingdom as interior values, they can more aptly recognize Jesus as the King of their lives.

WHAT IS THE GOSPEL?

I like to define the gospel as the Story of God's will, way, and work of providing salvation and justice through the gift of his Son Jesus for all of humanity. God's *will* is that the world be restored to its intended wholeness. This means that our union with God, which God created for us and shared with us, might be brought back to its initial state. God's *way* of providing salvation is through the message, mission, and means of Jesus. God's *work* of providing salvation and justice is through the people of God, the church, and—for our conversation—our youth ministries.

There is hefty controversy surrounding the gospel these days—and there has been throughout history. We could raise many issues, but the one that concerns me most is where the gospel has its origin. I believe it's what matters most to the life of our students as they engage in the mission and work of God as ministers of reconciliation. Since most associations with the term *gospel* have connections to the book of Isaiah, I believe the very core of the gospel is the message of restoration and healing.

I contend that the most helpful place to see a picture of the gospel is Luke 4:14-21. Jesus is only a few days into his earthly ministry when he returns to his hometown of Nazareth and is rejected. Luke 4:14-21 says:

> Jesus returned to Galilee in the power of the Spirit, and news about him spread through the whole countryside. He was teaching in their synagogues, and everyone praised him. He went to Nazareth, where he had been brought up, and on the Sabbath day he went into the synagogue, as was his custom. He stood up to read, and the scroll of the prophet Isaiah was handed to him. Unrolling it, he found the place where it is written: "The Spirit of the Lord is on me, because he has anointed me to proclaim *good news* to the *poor*. He has sent me to proclaim freedom for the *prisoners* and recovery of sight for the *blind*, to set the *oppressed* free, to proclaim the year of the Lord's favor." Then he rolled up the scroll, gave it back to the attendant and sat down. The eyes of everyone in the synagogue were fastened on him. He began by saying to them, "Today this scripture is fulfilled in your hearing." (*emphasis added*)

There is a lot we could say about this passage, and we'll be coming back to it in chapter 8. But for the purpose of discovering the key elements of the gospel in which to help our students realize how they're implicated in God's Story, I wish to simply look at two things.

First, I want you to remember that this passage has its roots in Isaiah 61:1-2.[72] Its most clearly illustrated point is that Jesus has come to "proclaim good news." Jesus has come to call people to a new way of life—a kingdom way of life that transcends an early reign on earth and flows into both an inner reign within his followers and a heavenly reign.

Second, I believe it's important to note that after Jesus proclaims why he's come, he makes a list of the people he's come to preach the good news to: (1) The poor, (2) prisoners, (3) the blind, and (4) the oppressed. And each of these four people groups is in need of both a spiritual restoration and a physical restoration.

The *poor* are truly poor—they have the fewest resources, but they're also spiritually poor, meaning they're without a restoring relationship with God. *Prisoners* refers to those held captive by Rome. (At this time in history, Rome ruled the world and tyrannized the Jewish nation.) Yet they're also those being held captive by their sins, the very thing keeping them spiritually poor. Today's prisoners are those in society who are lonely. The *blind*, as with the poor and the captive, have both a spiritual deficiency as well as a physical disability. Jesus came to share the good news with those who are physically blind, as well as those who are spiritually lost. And finally, the *oppressed* are those who've been left on their own. They—like the other three people groups—are the social outcasts who are broken, bruised, exploited, and in need of physical, emotional, and spiritual healing.

People Groups in Luke 4	Distinctives of the People Groups
Poor	Least
Prisoners	Lonely
Blind	Lost
Oppressed	Left

The gospel is a story about restoration and healing. And Jesus clearly demonstrates that to us by his proclamation in Luke chapter 4.[73] Our youth ministries, therefore, have been previously given a work—the work of the gospel. That work is to bring about salvation and justice through restorative acts of love and blessing. Meaning, our youth ministries are primarily about *and church* one thing—helping restore people to God, to themselves, to others, and to the world.[74] If, therefore, our youth ministries are going to be places of inspiration, equipping, and challenge to live and love in the way of Jesus, then they must be communities full of students and adults who are working to participate with God in his mission to restore the world to its intended wholeness through redemptive actions. We might say that *restoration* is a blanket term for God's intended mission. We might also, therefore, say *redemption* (along with other theological essentials such as adoption, reconciliation, justification, sanctification, and so on) is one of the ways God is actively restoring. It is important to note that God does the restoring and redeeming but uses us as agents of his love and blessing to do it.

Helping Students Articulate the Gospel Story

One of the most challenging aspects in youth ministry today is helping our students understand the gospel. More challenging than that, perhaps, is helping our students articulate the gospel.[75] When I started in youth ministry more than a decade ago, teaching students to articulate their faith was easy. Anyone can learn to use a tract, just flipping through a few pages of a glossy booklet, even if the students didn't know what the gospel meant to them or to others. A simple picture of a distressed stick figure standing on the side of a great chasm in need of a bridge was easy to draw on a napkin or a piece of notebook paper. A multicolored bracelet that illustrated the glory of God, sin, blood, new birth, faith, new life, and the kingdom of heaven was easy to wear and share—even if the students had no idea what it truly represented. Even though I no longer believe that tracts or napkin drawings or bracelets are the best way to explain the gospel, who Jesus is, or how to know Jesus personally, I do believe it's still essential that we help our students learn how to articulate the gospel Story.

Actually, if I am completely honest, I don't think the techniques I just listed above are really all that inherently bad or ineffective. In some ways using these types of things is no different than what I'm about to show you, or displaying a Celtic cross tattoo, or wearing a cross hanging around my neck. No, the issue isn't the symbolism or the illustration of the techniques; it's what's *behind* the techniques that concerns me. I don't particularly like the content of most tracts. The gospel that's presented in most booklets or pamphlets doesn't account for a full narrative view of God—the kingdom, restoration, justice, and salvation. Instead, it presents a view that's constricted and just too neat and clean. But regardless of the content, I'm much more concerned by the narrow propositional approach, the elitist attitude, and the lack of understanding that's often behind the easy use of a booklet.

If students are truly reaching out to other students through restorative acts of justice and compassion, then at some point a conversation about the Story of God and the gospel will inevitably come up. Francis of Assisi said, "Preach the gospel at all times and when necessary use words." I totally agree with the spirit in which he made that statement. However, some use this statement to support the idea that we don't need to use words to tell the Story of God. That just isn't true. Perhaps we don't need to use *only* words, and oftentimes using words first is the *worst* thing we can do. But we can't deny that the main way people communicate with one another is through words. Our students are always using words via text messages, email, Facebook, phone calls, or just normal everyday conversations. Words, when appropriately used, can be very helpful.

I've been using a really simple way to help my students articulate the Story of God. (See the four circles below.) As with any method of sharing your faith, if it's used outside of relationships, without context, and to state emphatic propositions through imposition, then it won't be effective. On the other hand, if it's used fittingly and correctly, this method can help your students share the Story of God—and ultimately their own story.

Please don't make a tract or other formulaic resource out of this. Instead, just use it to help your students know how to better tell the Story of God— the stories of what God has done and is doing in their lives.

God **DESIGNED** the world to be full of life. God's creation was good and whole. Humans were a special part of God's design. Humans were created to live in perfect relationship with God and to care for the earth. Humans were also created to worship God by living under God's rule.	Humans rejected God by choosing to be their own god. The perfect relationship with God was **BROKEN,** and the world was no longer whole. Because of their choice to sin, humans were separated from God, and the whole world was no longer a perfect place. We call this separation death. Because of his love, God made a promise with humans that would mend the broken world.	God's promise was fulfilled when Jesus came to the earth to live with humans. Jesus was God. Jesus **SATISFIED** the punishment of death for humans. Jesus' death on a cross, his burial in a grave, and his resurrection from that grave gives humans a chance to experience a mended relationship with God, no longer separated by death but joined together by a new life, moving toward a whole world. Jesus not only died for humans, but he also showed humans how to live under the rule of God, no longer living as if they are their own god.	As humans believe by faith that God is the ruler of life and believe that Jesus' death, burial, and resurrection provided the way for salvation, they experience God's restoration. One day the perfect relationship that God intended to have with humans will be **RESTORED.** God's creation will one day be good and made completely whole. Humans will dwell with God; and as the ruler of life, God will be worshipped for all time.

If we want our students to understand how they're implicated in the Story of God so they might participate with God to restore his world, then they'll have to know what the gospel is and how to tell the Story of the gospel. Of course, this doesn't negate the need for them to actively live out the gospel as well. The gospel Story must be proclaimed and performed.

I think one reason the illustration above is so helpful for our students is because it doesn't begin with the fall of humanity. Rather, it begins with a world that was designed as whole. The wholeness of the world included the imago Dei, or the image of God. Humanity was designed in the likeness of God and was an integral part of the world God declared "good." I believe it is much more helpful to teach our students to articulate a faith that doesn't begin with how bad someone is. I wonder if students helping students see how close they are to God is more helpful than students helping students know how far they are from God. It isn't just semantics. The Story of God didn't begin with brokenness; it began with a world that was good, right, and whole. Helping students articulate a full narrative view of God is essential to not-yet believers understanding the true nature of God and the gospel Story. Students already know they are "fallen." Let's help them know how good and whole they might become.

The Gospel for a Postmodern Mindset

Before Stanley Grenz died, I was able to share a meal with him during a Youth Specialties conference in San Diego.[76] I'm deeply indebted to Stan for his many creative works, but also for taking the time to help me rethink how the gospel needs to be articulated for a postmodern mindset.

That day Stan spent more than an hour helping me to see that a relevant gospel for a postmodern culture must be characterized in four ways.[77] First, the gospel must be *post-individualistic*. Simply stated: The gospel is best understood and proclaimed in community. This is true because the gospel is communal. It isn't about you or me—it's about us. Postmoderns believe that knowledge is wrought through cognitive frameworks mediated by the communities in which they participate. Grenz says, "With its focus on community, the postmodern world encourages us to recognize the importance of the community of faith in our evangelistic efforts. Members of the next generation are often unimpressed by our verbal presentations of the gospel."[78] This means it's very important to make sure that our students aren't articulating the gospel only with their mouths, but also with their lives. The best apologetic of the gospel is one's life, not mere words.

A community of people who are living and loving in the ways of Jesus and who recognize the importance of a post-individualistic gospel can help the rising generations have encounters with God. Inviting postmodern students into a community whose first priority is to reveal God through Jesus will draw others to Jesus in the communal embodiment of the gospel in the authentic community they share.[79]

Second, the gospel must be *post-rationalistic*. This means that the elevation of reason found in modernism is irrelevant to postmoderns today. A postmodern articulation of the gospel no longer focuses on mere propositions as the central tenet of the Christian faith. On the other hand, a postmodern articulation of the gospel is equally serious about the dynamic dimensions of human experience and the attempts of each person to make the most sense out of life.[80]

Third, a postmodern articulation of the gospel must be *post-dualistic*. We've talked about this concept quite a bit in this book already, so I'll be brief here. The gospel cannot separate the soul from the body. Rather, the gospel in a postmodern context must be about a unified whole that includes the whole of a person. A gospel for today's students, as we've already mentioned, cannot solely focus on saving souls. Rather, it must genuinely seek to restore the whole person to a society of God. Finding union with God and true relationship with ourselves and with others must become a more common call to true conversion of broken images of God to newly designed images of God.

Finally, articulating the gospel for postmoderns, according to Grenz, must be *post-noeticentric*. (Yeah, I wasn't sure that was a real word when Grenz spoke it either, but I guess it is.) The word *noeticentric*, as Grenz uses it, means that our gospel must become more than the collection of knowledge.[81] The gospel must serve as the gathering of not only intellectual smarts, but also wisdom that leads to Christian formation. A post-noeticentric gospel doesn't allow for the amassing of propositions alone, but it does push for a changed heart. Therefore, knowledge isn't for intellectualism's sake but for the sake of conforming more to the mission, message, and means of Jesus.

The gospel must be articulated—in words and actions—for it to be relevant to a postmodern culture. Helping our students understand this necessity and giving them a narrative to begin to articulate and a lens in which to view the gospel is imperative to a youth ministry that's leaning into and living out the goals of God's mission—salvation and justice.

WHAT IS THE CHURCH?

You may already know that the word *church* comes from the Greek word *ecclesia,* which means "called-out ones" or "an assembly." You may also know that the church isn't merely a structure of some kind but a gathering of believers, often referred to as "the body of Christ" (Ephesians 1:22-23).[82]

Typically, the body of Christ is described as being comprised of two aspects: The universal church and the local church. The universal church simply refers to all people who've decided to let Jesus be the King of their lives and have a restoring relationship with Jesus. In other words, the universal church is anyone who's received salvation.

The local church is a smaller expression of the larger universal, and it's your personal faith community. It's through the local or neighborhood church that the work of God happens on a profoundly relational level. God's mission is fulfilled through the work of the church or, more specifically, through the work of our youth ministries.

If the gospel is the Story of God's will, way, and work of providing salvation and justice through the gift of his Son Jesus for all of humanity, then it's through the church (or our youth ministries) that the Story becomes made physical and real to the world. True, there is essence to the church, but there is also tangibility.

I would venture to say that most students don't see themselves as the church but as people who go to church. If we truly want to make a change in the world, then we have to reverse that thinking and help students more fully understand the work of the church. One of the ways we can do that is to bring explicit definition to the purpose of the church. We can't assume that our students—or even our adult leaders—know the purpose of the church. Therefore, we ought to do everything we can to help our students and fellow youth workers realize the function of faith communities, both local and universal.

The following three roles of the church (and of our youth ministries) are integral to the fruitful accomplishment of God's mission. The church is to be a people of *conversion, community,* and *conformity.*

By *conversion* I don't just mean people who are saving souls. (I believe we've already covered the importance of a holistic element in our youth ministries throughout this book.) Conversion is a true renovation of the soul, heart, mind, and body. Youth ministries that are fruitfully doing the work of God are seeking to be places or people of conversion. A people of conversion are concerned with evangelism, hospitality, openness, formation, generosity, and liberation. These qualities combine to create an environment in which people are welcomed to join others in the process of restoration.

By *community* I mean people (or youth ministry) who are providing a sense of belonging to a world that's often left to find its own sense of faith, hope, and love. Youth ministries that diligently do the work of God are gathering places in which relationships are a high priority. They're gathering places where people walk through life with one another in meaningful ways, entering into the joy, celebration, suffering, and pain of others. A youth ministry that offers genuine community is a sharing community, making sure that no one is in need and that people within the community don't partake at the detriment of others. Youth ministries committed to community are profoundly marked by inclusiveness.

By *conformity* I mean that youth ministries are a society of people known for their desire to form spiritually. We'll talk much more about areas of formation in chapter 8. But for the purpose of closing this chapter, let me suggest that a faith community interested in conformity is a community that's consistently seeking to arrange its personal and communal lives around the mission of God, the person and work of Jesus, and submission to the ministry gifts and roles of the Holy Spirit in order to become people who are full of grace and dedicated to the healing of all people through salvation and justice.

Reflection and Discussion Questions:

Chapter 6—Implication: God's Story as the Context for Our Identity and Calling

• Pretend you're invited to speak to the adults of your church. How would you describe yourself? Take a moment and write a "paragraph of introduction" that describes your identity. Be sure to write about who you are, not just what you do.

• Referring to the list of the Five Factors of personality (on pages 99-100), which do you align with most closely?

• In what ways are you helping the students in your youth ministry celebrate the divergent identities and personality traits that make up the composition of your youth ministry?

• Chapter 6 suggests there are two types of calling: The general calling is to be about the mission of God, while the specific calling is our unique contribution to the mission of God. What is your specific calling in life?

• What about Jesus' person and work most inspires you? In what ways do you remain attentive to those things for your own spiritual discovery and growth?

• How would you define the gospel?

• Chapter 6 suggests there are challenging factors in training students how to articulate their faith in today's context. What other factors would you say contribute to the challenge of training students in how to articulate their faith?

- On a scale of 1 to 10, with 10 being the most, how helpful is the story approach to helping students find a starting point to articulating their faith? What would you suggest as a way to improve the illustration?

- Chapter 6 suggests that there are three primary roles of the church— conversion, community, and conformity. What other roles would be helpful to add to this list?

CHAPTER 7
Integration: God's Story as the Context for Our Way of Life

Out of the Story of God comes revelation. From a fuller understanding of God, our theological foundation is built. This theological foundation helps us understand our identity and our calling. A discovery of our identity and calling leads us into the process of developing a way of life.

All that students have come to know about the things of God now begin to be integrated. From the image in which they were created, to the basis for practical theology, to the ability to articulate the gospel, students begin to synthesize all that they've come to know in order to develop a set of beliefs and virtues that shape the way they live.[83]

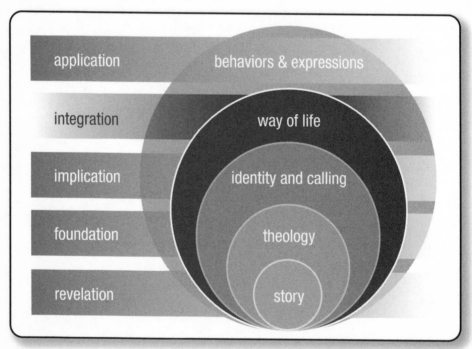

Long before the process of integration begins, the idea of being a disciple emerged and most likely took hold in students' lives. However, it's at this stage of their development that students realize there is more to being a follower of Jesus than ideas about God. Even with the ability to take the ideas of God and make them tangible, students take one step further and begin assembling a set of core beliefs. This core ideology comes out of the understanding that a disciple is more than a student of Jesus. "A disciple is one who engages with Jesus as a person and, by trusting in him, begins to live out the virtues that Jesus talks about."[84]

Simply said, a disciple must go beyond ideas and implement practices. But before students can effectively do this, they must have a creed by which to live, one that governs their thoughts and begins to develop a set of virtues that will provide for their theological foundations to become deeply personal. For it's out of a creed that a student's behavior and expressions of God will eventually be displayed. (We'll talk about the application of God's Story through behaviors and expressions in the next chapter.)

I read *The Jesus Creed* by Scot McKnight several years ago. (Scot also wrote the foreword to this book, in case you missed it.) Scot is a professor at North Park University near Chicago, Illinois, and a prolific author of books and blog posts. Scot is also providing a sense of balance to all that is happening today as it relates to the emerging church conversation.

Anyway, it was in Scot's *Jesus Creed* book that I was introduced to the above definition of a disciple. I was so in love with the book that I just had to talk with him about it. So I contacted Scot and asked him if we could meet to discuss his book. (By this time I think I'd single-handedly accounted for the sale of more than 1,000 copies of his book!)

Scot agreed to meet with me over lunch near the North Park campus. After an hour or so of meaningful conversation, I finally got around to asking, "So, what are the virtues of Jesus? In your definition of a disciple, you claim that a disciple is one who lives out the virtues of Jesus. What are those virtues?"

Scot replied something to the effect of, "You scour the gospels. You do the work of discovering for yourself what the virtues of Jesus are. After you feel like you've discovered them, call me and we'll set up another time to meet and discuss what you think the virtues of Jesus are."

I was hoping to receive the formula that day. But what I *did* get was the privilege of doing the hard work of going through the Gospels with a fine-tooth comb and discovering the creed of Jesus, as I understood it. Scot's book was a great starting point for me as I realized that organizing the entire life of Jesus would be difficult to do if I didn't at least have two big buckets to put them into. The two buckets for identifying the virtues of

Jesus came from Jesus' commandments to (1) love God and (2) love others. Another way to look at it is the inward formation of Jesus and the outward formation of Jesus.

I'd encourage each of you to take the time to scour the Gospels and create your own list. For the purpose of this book, I'll provide you with what I came up with, but don't let that discourage you from engaging in and learning from the process of study and discovery. In doing so, you might choose to record 8 or 10 or 20 of the same or different virtues of Jesus. I believe it's fine that each of us understands the life, voice, and actions of Jesus from different angles. The point isn't so much from what angle you view Jesus and the virtues that shaped his life, but that you've worked to discover the list of virtues and you begin to live them out.

It's important to note here that you'll need to facilitate an exercise of some sort that helps your students discover the virtues of Jesus. Don't just pass these along to your students. If they don't experience the practice of seeking the virtues of Jesus on their own, then their levels of Intersection and Identification won't go as deep.

Here are the six virtues of Jesus' life, voice, and actions that I discovered through my Gospels dive. I hope they serve as a springboard for your own discovery.

Inward Formation - Love God	Outward Formation - Love Others
Surrender	Reveal Truth
Abide	Restore Community
Reflect	Impart Life

JESUS' VIRTUES OF LOVING GOD

We observe in Jesus' life a commitment to living the first Great Commandment. Jesus modeled what it means to "love the Lord your God with all your heart and with all your soul and with all your mind and with all your strength" (Mark 12:30). At the center of Jesus' life was a deep love for his Father. He was constantly aware of how much God loved him. In Scripture Jesus was the first to call God *Abba*, which means "daddy" or "papa."

He knew God in deep ways, and he lived in the reality of this love. We're offered the same chance to know God as our "Abba"—to draw close and pour out our hearts to him. God desires to love us and to receive our love in response.

Jesus modeled what it means to *surrender.*

Jesus gives us the perfect picture of what it means to surrender to God. Out of Jesus' deep love for his Father, he gave over and resigned his life to God.

Jesus understood his need to completely depend on the Father. He followed God's plan all the way to his death on a cross. In the midst of his agony, Jesus knew he belonged to God and could fully depend on him. We also express our love to God when we give our lives over to him, which involves completely surrendering to God and abandoning our old ways.

The call to follow Jesus is a call to "death" and abandoning the old way of life; it also involves rebirth. When we fully surrender our lives to Jesus, he makes us into new people, calling us to be part of a new community that has access to God's supernatural guidance and strength. It's out of this supernatural strength and guidance that our desire to surrender our lives and be like Christ in our world emerges and is unremitting.

Jesus modeled what it means to *abide.*

Jesus abided with the Father, growing close to God by continually making time for him, even though Jesus was surrounded by the many needs of the demanding crowds who pursued him.

To love someone means to long to be with that person. Jesus longed to be with God, and he looked at abiding as an act of love. He wanted to know God's thoughts and heart. He also realized how much he needed God's strength to get him through his life on earth.

To abide means to journey with, to dwell, or to sojourn. Jesus calls us to journey with him, remaining in his love and living in the awareness of his presence.

Jesus modeled what it means to *reflect* the very nature of God.

Jesus was the full expression of God here on earth. Jesus displayed many of the attributes of God, therefore revealing the heart of God. His hope, grace, compassion, love, justice, righteousness, and so on that are seen in the Gospels are a reflection of God and his very nature and attributes.

To reflect is to be recognized by the characteristics of another, to show an image of, or to mirror. Our call is to embrace the new life and way that we've received from God through Jesus, and in doing so we'll reveal to the world the heart of God.

The Holy Spirit guides us and helps us become more like Jesus—but this doesn't happen automatically. We must choose to surrender to the Holy Spirit who lives within us, moment by moment. The strength and guidance of God is always available to us; we must choose to rely on him.

Often people see the "reflect" virtue as one that is more about the outward than the inward. But reflecting the nature of God doesn't begin on the outside. What is inside of us is where the reflection of God, seen from others on the outside, begins.

THE CALL TO LIVE OUT THE VIRTUES OF JESUS

In Mark 1:15-18, Jesus calls his followers to obey three directives: *repent, believe,* and *follow* (also found in Matthew 4:18-22, Luke 5:2-11, and John 1:35-42).

> "The time has come," he said, "The kingdom of God has come near. Repent and believe the good news!" As Jesus walked beside the Sea of Galilee, he saw Simon and his brother Andrew casting a net into the lake, for they were fishermen. "Come, follow me," Jesus said, "and I will send you out to fish for people." At once they left their nets and followed him.

The call to repent, believe, and follow is an ongoing practice in the life of a maturing follower of Jesus. This transformational process can help us become like Jesus in the way we surrender to God, abide in God, and reflect the nature of God.

Repent (Surrender) To repent is to turn away from something with the intentions of never returning. Repentance involves recognizing our sin, confessing our sin and releasing it, and receiving forgiveness from God.

Believe (Abide) To believe is to trust or have faith. We abide when we believe in Jesus, embrace him as truth, and demonstrate his character and priorities.

Follow (Reflect) To follow is to imitate. Jesus called us not just to a life of pursuing or chasing him, but imitating him. Imitating Jesus is a life in pursuit of holiness, surrendering to the Holy Spirit. We imitate Jesus when our relationship with him leads us to *increase the frequency and duration of the holy moments in our lives.* These moments bring us to a deeper union with God.

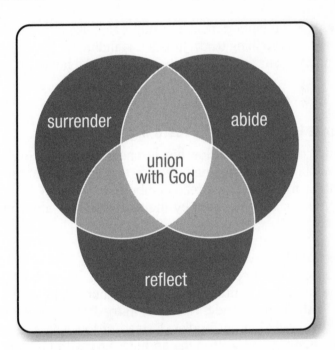

JESUS' VIRTUES OF LOVING OTHERS

We observe in Jesus' life a passionate commitment to the second Great Commandment. Jesus models what it means to "love your neighbor as yourself." When we experience the perfect love of God, it changes our perspective on life, each other, and ourselves. We become motivated to share this love inside of us. We look to Jesus as our example of how we should love each other.

Jesus shows love to others by *revealing truth.*

Jesus continually revealed truth through his life, words, and actions; and God has given us an amazing responsibility to represent him and reveal his truth by being humbly present in the lives of others.

Revealing God's truth begins with how we live. The most important thing you can share with someone is your life, and our lives must support the gospel message we're trying to share with others.

Because Jesus is the embodiment of truth, being like him means we must exercise justice in revealing truth. Justice is standing for fairness and equality. It's a commitment to bring dignity to, serve, and honor all people.

Jesus shows love to others by *restoring a community.*

Jesus called a community to follow him in a new way of life. He was redeeming this community by calling them to a life that was different from the one so many of his followers had already embraced—Judaism. Ultimately, this community would be redeemed by the work of Jesus' atonement on the cross.

As followers of Christ, we're part of this redeemed community. We're the continuation of God's Story—the body of Christ being led by the Holy Spirit to be the physical presence of Jesus in our world. In an authentic way, Jesus is still here in body. However, instead of physically walking on this earth, he "walks" in our bodies. Instead of touching and smiling and crying and laughing and welcoming and listening with his own two eyes, hands, and ears, Jesus does so through one body composed of millions of his followers!

God has given each of us a new identity and a unique calling in his church. Together, we have a remarkable responsibility to create a community filled with God's love and truth.

Jesus shows love to others by *imparting life* to them.

Jesus is the ultimate expression of God's love and care for us. The incarnation of Jesus shows us just how much God loves us and wants to give us life. Just as Jesus gave his life for us, we must impart life to others by giving away our lives. Following Jesus' compassionate way, we must slow down enough to be fully present with people, walking alongside them, listening, caring, serving—giving our lives away for their sakes.

In Jesus Christ we see the fullness of God's compassion. In *Compassion: A Reflection on the Christian Life*, Donald McNeill, Henri Nouwen, and Douglas Morrison write—

> To us, who cry out from the depth of our brokenness for a hand that will touch us, an arm that can embrace us, lips that will kiss us, a word that speaks to us here and now, and a heart that is not afraid of our fears and tremblings; to us, to feel our own pain as no other human being feels it...and who are always waiting for someone who dares to come close—to us a person has come who could truly say, "I am with you." Jesus Christ, who is God-with-us, has come to us in the freedom of love, not needing to experience our human condition but freely choosing to do so out of love.[85]

Giving away your life involves being aware of all that God has given to you (gifts, wisdom, talents, experiences, and so on) and being willing to use those things for the benefit of others, laying aside your own pursuits and self-seeking desires. Giving your life away means you're available to live in the proximity of others and to be intentional about spending time investing in the development of others. This investment requires that we help others know how to live in the ways of Jesus and share in his mission.

OUR CALL TO LIVE OUT THE VIRTUES OF JESUS

> Then Jesus came to them and said, "All authority in heaven and on earth has been given to me. Therefore go and make disciples of all nations, baptizing them in the name of the Father and of the Son and of the Holy Spirit, and teaching them to obey everything I have commanded you. And surely I am with you always, to the very end of the age." (Matthew 28:18-20)

In the Great Commission, we make three important observations of Jesus' call to his followers to make disciples.

Go(ing)—Revealing Truth: Entering into and engaging in the lives of others by inviting and welcoming them into the journey of following and experiencing Jesus. (Matthew 4:19, Mark 1:17, Luke 5:27, John 1:43)

Jesus revealed truth by entering into and engaging with culture. Jesus progressively invited and welcomed people to enter into the journey of following him. In fact, his invitations never ceased. From early on in his ministry and even after his death, burial, and resurrection, we find Jesus inviting people to follow him.

Jesus was passionate about sharing and showing the "evangel"—the good news we commonly refer to as "the gospel story" and from which we get the word *evangelism*. Jesus even proclaims that the core truth of the gospel is the reason for his incarnation—"to seek and to save what was lost" (Luke 19:10) and "to proclaim good news to the poor" (Luke 4:18-19).

Baptizing—Restoring a Community: Calling others to identify with Jesus' cause and his community of followers, the body of Christ. (Matthew 7:28; 8:16-17; Mark 1:2, 32-34; Luke 4:32, 40-41)

In order that his followers might understand and identify with his person and work, trusting him and developing a new life in him, Jesus called into being a community that would assist his followers with their spiritual formation. The inward and outward formation of his followers was imperative to Jesus' mission and explicit in his ways of teaching, such as parables, stories, figures of speech, blessings and curses, as well as through his healing and sign miracles.

As a part of the disciples' formation and ministry experiences, Jesus equipped his community with the perspective to meet the people's needs. The disciples used what they'd learned from Jesus as they were sent out to invite and welcome people into the journey of following him. Partway through Jesus' earthly ministry, we see his followers becoming like him as they participated in his mission "to seek and to save what was lost" (Luke 19:10) by entering into and engaging in the lives of others.

Teaching—Imparting Life: Equipping others to embrace Jesus' way of life and to contribute to his mission. (Matthew 10:1-42, Mark 6:7-11, Luke 9:1-5)

Jesus appointed twelve of his followers and began investing in and imparting his life to them. Jesus then sent out the Twelve so they might continue to call others to a new way of life and mission.

PARALLEL EXECUTION

The inward and outward formation in our lives has to happen in parallel execution, which means these two areas of formation are inseparable—you don't do one without the other. We can't choose which one we like better and then live by only that one. A virtuous life in the way of Jesus is about the identification of and, ultimately, the working out of both inward and outward formation, in chorus. Parallel execution leads us to *Emmanualism*,[86] the practice of living and loving in the way of Jesus. It's revealing God's intended ways through our character and community, our compassion and justice, our conversation and stories, and our celebration and worship.

Our students need help discovering the virtues of Jesus. Our students need you and me to be a living observation of what it means to be committed to Emmanualism, the inward and outward formation of our lives.

Reflection and Discussion Questions
Chapter 7—Integration: God's Story as the Context for Our Way of Life

• What do you think of the following definition of a disciple? "A disciple is one who engages with Jesus as a person and, by trusting in him, begins living out the virtues that Jesus talks about."

• What might be missing from the list of virtues in the Inward and Outward Formation chart (on page 122)?

• Take a moment to go back and read the quote from Henri Nouwen and his coauthors on page 127. As you read, circle the words that are important to you. In what ways are you being a humble presence in the lives of your students?

• In what ways are you revealing truth to the world around you?

• In what ways are you restoring the people around you to an authentic community?

• In what ways are you imparting life to your students? How might you more effectively do this?

PART THREE: SACRED RHYTHMS

To be sacred means to be deeply spiritual and consecrated (set apart) for the devotion to some greater purpose. To be sacred is to be holy, devout, and saintly. To have sacred rhythms, therefore, means to have a patterned recurrence of holy, devout, or saintly actions in our lives. And these actions are marks that evidence a desired life of harmonious movements that provide cadence for our behaviors and practices.

We're called to be saintly people—people who've been set apart from the movements of the world and therefore marked with holiness—a devout life. There are two aspects of this devout life. First, there's an individual holiness that we're to strive to complete. Second, there's a communal holiness that the people of God, the church, are to embrace and subsequently endorse through their way of life. These actions set us apart from the world, bringing due glory to God. These various actions or behaviors and practices prove to the world around us that we, in fact, are agents of God's love and blessing—restoration.

Sacred rhythms explore the interrelatedness between principles and experience. Sacred rhythms substantiate that, as agents of God's restorative activity, what we say we believe and what we actually live out match up. This is how the goals of God's mission—salvation and justice—are best lived out. We carry out God's mission when we journey to God's cadence call.

Our students need us to guide them toward behaviors and expressions that grow out of their way of life and reveal and accomplish the work of God. In the next two chapters we'll look at various behaviors and practices that are essential to a missional life and to a missional youth ministry. We'll look at specific ways that God's mission is wrought, helping us measure our effectiveness as missional communities that are passionately committed to being the will, way, and work of providing salvation and justice to the world through God's Son, Jesus.

Furthermore, these behaviors and expressions aren't only for *now*. They're designed to help students lean into and live out God's mission long after our immediate influence and impact on their lives is finished. As you well know, youth ministry isn't about a product; it's about a process. And these behaviors and expressions are about providing a process for students to engage now and work out forever.

In the words of Eugene Peterson:

> The end, for Christians, is God's work of salvation. This is a salvation understood as comprehensive, intricate, patiently personal, embracingly social, insistently political. Salvation is the work of God that restores the world and us to wholeness. God's work complete. Glory. Eternal life. And we are in on it, in on the redemption of the world. Whoever I am, and wherever I find myself in history, in geography, in "sickness or in health," in whatever circumstance, I am in the middle of it, God's work of salvation. "Kingdom of God" is Jesus' term for it. This is what is going on.[87]

Peterson goes on to note the means of this salvation, "In one word, Jesus. Jesus, pure and simple."[88] If we're going to call students to actively contribute to the mission, message, and means of Jesus with salvation as the goal, then we must help them establish a life that applies all they've come to know and experience to living out the appropriate expressions of Jesus to the whole world.

It's out of the stories of God that we understand who God is (revelation), a theological basis (foundation) for knowing and experiencing God, the context and meaning of our identity and calling (implication), a way or rule of life (integration) that flows out of all that we know and become in order that we might have a set of behaviors and expressions (application) that in the end completes the work of God—salvation and justice.

Along with an understanding of the individual behaviors and expressions that are essential to developing Story-formed students are the essential characteristics of a Story-formed community. The next two chapters will help us construct a framework for developing Story-formed students that includes how we understand Christian formation, developing and sustaining creative environments, and the specific roles youth workers play as they seek to share experiences of spiritual growth and discovery with students.

CHAPTER 8

Application: God's Story as the Context for Our Behaviors and Expressions

Out of the development of a set of beliefs and virtues that provide for the ongoing means of shaping one's life emerge specific behaviors and expressions. These are what mark the follower of Jesus as one who is Story-formed.

The narrative of God provides a glimpse into the heart of God, revealing his mission. God's enduring mission clearly and boldly reveals to us the longing he has for his work to be done "on earth as it is in heaven" (Matthew 6:10).

Before we talk about the specific behaviors and expression that Story-formed students live out, it's imperative that we first develop a list of traits that comprise the Story-formed communities from which Story-formed students will be developed.

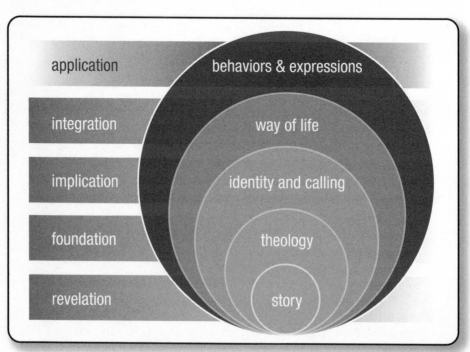

DESCRIBING A STORY-FORMED COMMUNITY

There are, generally speaking, four different models of youth ministry. Obviously, there are uniquenesses within each youth ministry's church and community contexts that provide variation to the models. However, if you take a moment to look around your immediate area and the region where you're doing youth work, I believe you'll agree with me that there are four main models of youth ministry.

The four models traditionally executed throughout North America are—

1. The social-oriented model

2. The attractional model

3. The externally focused model

4. The narrative-missional model

Of course, in this book I'm trying to make a case for the narrative-missional model because I believe it's out of the narrative of God that we're introduced to and called into active participation in the mission of God.

There's nothing inherently good or bad in these four. Like in any other type of model (education, business, and so on), the effectiveness doesn't hinge on the structure as much as it does on the people who are implementing the model. With that said, however, I believe there are some philosophical shortcomings that cause models to fail, regardless of the style of effectiveness or the people implementing them.

Humor me for a minute and take a look at the first three models. Then we'll take an in-depth look at the narrative-missional model.

Social-Oriented Model

This model is about providing a place for students to feel welcomed and like they belong. There is a desire for Jesus to be known, accepted, and lived out; but the primary mechanism for growth is activity and recreation. Therefore, either little formation occurs or the formation that does occur in the four major areas of evangelism, justice, discipleship, and community is only partial.

Some social-oriented models spend most of their time engaging social justice issues and seeking to build relationships with students through these events. This model typically measures its effectiveness in the number of people served. The social-oriented model isn't bad. And with appropriate leadership, it can really help a lot of people. In my opinion, however, this model fails because it doesn't hit on all four areas of formation.

The Attractional Model

This model's primary focus is attracting a crowd of students through an array of tools and toys, such as concerts, creatively designed spaces, climbing walls, gaming systems, game tables, and so on. The end goal isn't just to attract students, but to try to make disciples of students. However, as I've observed, there's often so much energy given to attracting the students that there's little time, staff, or money left over for anything else. The common thinking is, *If I can just get them here, then we can convince them of Jesus.* This model typically measures its effectiveness by the number of students attending programs, activities, and events.

The attractions aren't bad in and of themselves, as you know. I mean, who doesn't want a boatload of students coming into their ecosystem? However, when youth ministries primarily focus on getting kids in the door, they also, like the social-oriented model, fail to help students form spiritually in all four areas of Christian formation.

The Externally Focused Model

This model seeks to identify the needs of the students and families in the community and begins its ministry there. The emphasis is service. Leadership works extremely hard to develop a reputation in the community as the go-to people for whatever needs the ministry addresses. This model is interested in getting students to serve others and do service projects. Many of these types of ministries deal with particular issues, such as eating disorders, alcohol and drug addiction, or school-based needs like tutoring. This model typically measures its effectiveness by the influence it's having in the community, as well as the number of people served.

Again, as with the other two models, there's nothing wrong with it. The goal is to introduce people to Jesus, and most often the spirit behind the serving is, *Well, even if we didn't get to tell a student about Jesus, we did get to help teenagers heal in some way.* What could be bad about that? However, this model doesn't give attention to all four areas of Christian formation either. Therefore, in my opinion, it fails.

The Narrative-Missional Model

This model is about developing Story-formed students who live as missionaries. It's a model that works hard to keep all four areas of Christian formation in mind and practice. Like the other three, it's very much about engaging in the lives of people. Students in this model are inspired to lean into the narrative of God and live out the mission of God in ways that are unique to them. The students in this model are equipped to "live" among the lost students in their schools, at work, on their teams, and so on, and decidedly choose to love them and learn from them.

This model of youth ministry measures its effectiveness by its faithfulness to the mission and work of God and by the type of people it forms. Numbers of people served, the number of people who attend, and the amount of influence this type of youth ministry might garner are important but secondary to the type of students it sends out.

Along with the above traits of a narrative-missional model, you'll also find the following characteristics. (Note: I realize I'm not being fair to the other models by not also listing their characteristics. However, my point here isn't to prove the ineffectiveness of other models as much as it is to highlight the outcomes and distinctive characteristics of the narrative-missional model.)

- *Incarnational*—living with students and amid their needs

- *Missiological*—about the mission and work of God's grand narrative

- *Character-concerned*—concerned about not only their students' outward appearance, but also their interior lives

- *Contextual*—made appropriately available to the people living in the community

- *Theological*—committed to the doctrines of God—all of them—in narrative fashion

- *Organic*—develops naturally and avoids the synthetic things that come quickly and fade even quicker

- *Multicultural*—recognizes the diversity of others and seeks to inspire students with a passion for the various ethnic groups in their community

- *Presence-centered*—seeks to find ways to connect students to God and help them center their lives around him (See the section on "Time, Space, and Matter" in chapter 9.)

- *Healthy community*—a group of common people sharing life with one another

- *Wholeness*—concerned about the wellness of their students' entire beings, including the spiritual, physical, emotional, intellectual, and sociological aspects

- *Spirit-yielded*—attentive to what the Spirit might be doing in the lives of students and in the life of the community; willing to obey the Spirit's leading over the leaders' preferences, opinions, dreams, and so on

- *Textual*—deeply committed to the Story of God and always looking for ways to help students develop their lives around the Bible

- *Prayerfully dependent*—relying on God through constant prayer to help them guide students into Christian formation

- *Hospitable*—an inviting and welcoming community marked by its generosity toward regulars as well as newcomers

- *Hope-filled*—trusting the power of Jesus to be and provide the hope of the world; always expecting that Jesus will heal the brokenness and be the source of a renewed life

- *Peace-filled*—trusting the power of Jesus to be and provide peace and harmony in a violent world, as well as in the hostile environments in which so many students live

- *Evangelistic*—committed to sharing the gospel in personal and communal ways

- *Justice*—seeking ways to bring dignity to all people and create an atmosphere of equality

- *People development*—committed to raising up a generation of students who will develop the next generation in missional living

Story-formed youth ministries diligently work hard to instill the above characteristics into the lives of the students they shepherd. If youth ministries are truly remaining committed to helping students lean into the narrative of God and live out the mission of God, then they'll develop Story-formed students.

DESCRIBING A STORY-FORMED STUDENT

After his death, burial, and resurrection, Jesus appeared to his disciples over a period of 40 days, convincing them that he was alive and teaching them about the kingdom of God.

Just before his ascension, Jesus told his followers not to leave Jerusalem and promised them that the Holy Spirit would be coming to baptize them (Acts 1:4-5). Jesus also gave his disciples a picture of what their responsibilities would be when the Spirit did come. His disciples would be given power by the Holy Spirit to be his witnesses (or storytellers). His disciples were to give an account or evidence of Jesus throughout Jerusalem, Judea, Samaria, and to the ends of the earth (Acts 1:8).

Upon painting this picture for his disciples, Jesus left the earth and ascended into heaven. Shortly afterward, the Holy Spirit came and entered into the disciples' community—just as Jesus had promised.

Along with Jesus' promise of the Holy Spirit (Acts 1:4-5) came power (Acts 1:8) and presence. And through the power of the Holy Spirit, the disciples were given the ability to embody the life of Jesus. Through the power *and* the presence of the Holy Spirit, the disciples formed a community that existed to serve and act as the extension of Jesus.

Our youth ministries are about trying to develop passionate students who will engage in the work of God and live as an extension of Jesus' mission as understood through Luke 4:17-21. We're consistently attempting to inspire the rising generations to be *storytellers*—God's witnesses. They're the people who give evidence of God by way of their lives, voices, and actions—their behaviors and expressions. We're trying to help our students nurture their interior lives and their exterior lives. The interior life deals with *discipleship* and *community*; the exterior life deals with *evangelism* and *justice*.

Storytellers who are concerned with the four areas of formation perform certain tasks as they give evidence to their behaviors and expressions. These storytellers seek to deliver context and meaning for the Story of God through a number of ways.

Yielding to the Cultural Context (or Audience) and the Environment

A storyteller knows how to adjust the Story to fit the audience and environment. The storyteller must be aware of the subtleties of the audience and the surroundings in which the Story is being told, adapting the telling of the Story to fit the listeners. We call this "contextualization," and this is a key aspect to any storyteller's inventory of characteristics.

Convening People Through a Spirit of Unity and Community

A storyteller has the ability to pull together the stories of all people in order to illustrate the divergences. However, equally important is discovering the details of each person's story that converge into a united whole that focuses on the similarities. This results in a community of people who see their differences yet celebrate them in the context of togetherness and harmony.

Inviting and Welcoming People to be a Part of the Story

The storyteller as witness calls others to be a part of the Story and receives them into the sharing of a unified whole. Inclusiveness is a major tenet of any storyteller's inventory of characteristics. The invitation is the easy part; it's the ongoing acceptance of people who may not be as interested in the Story that's hard. The storyteller as witness realizes that not everyone will be leaning forward into the Story, yet remains consistent in her invitation and welcoming of people regardless of who they are.

Offering Opportunities to Participate and Contribute to the Story

A storyteller offers herself to the audience. While an invitation calls for a response, an offering just is. Regardless of the listeners' responses, a storyteller seeks to engage them. Over and over and over again, if need be, storytellers seek to find ways to bring in opportunities to be a part of the Story and contribute to the Story's mission, hoping the immersion experience might lead to a deeper exploration of the Story.

Recognizing the Audience as a Significant Part of the Story

If there is no audience, then there's no need for the Story. Every effective storyteller realizes that the audience plays a huge role. So the storyteller treats the audience with respect, dignity, and care in order to allow the Story to be told and heard again. Recognizing the audience's role not only puts the role of the storyteller into perspective, but it also allows the audience to realize their significance.

LIFE FORMATION

Just as a storyteller has a set of tasks to perform while telling the Story, a storyteller witness must also be seeking to develop his interior and exterior life. The following are four indispensable areas of formation in the life of any storyteller.

Discipleship

Story-formed students will seek to live out the following behaviors and expressions:

- Spiritual disciplines such as prayer, study, simplicity, fasting, solitude, and so on

- Confession and repentance—telling God the truth about who they are and what they've done, while allowing that truth-telling experience to transform their lives

- Worship—expressing private, public, and communal ways to celebrate the Story of God

- Submission—obeying the teachings of Jesus as understood through the narrative of God

Community

I believe one of the best places to see the marks of true community in God's narrative is in 1 Corinthians 12:22-26, which says—

> On the contrary, those parts of the body that seem to be weaker are indispensable, and the parts that we think are less honorable we treat with *special honor*. And the parts that are unpresentable are treated with *special modesty*, while our presentable parts need *no special treatment*. But God has put the body together, giving *greater honor* to the parts that lacked it, so that there should be *no division* in the body, but that its parts should have *equal concern* for each other. If one part suffers, every part suffers with it; if one part is honored, every part *rejoices with it*. (*emphasis added*)

When students understand the nature of true community, they'll begin to live out the following behaviors and practices:

- "Special Honor": Lifting up the weaker students

- "Special Modesty": Protecting the defenseless students

- "No Special Treatment": Refusing privileges at the detriment of other students

- "Greater Honor": For those students who are never (or seldom) respected and valued

- "No Division": The greatest extent of harmony with others

- "Equal Concern": Treat other students as they want to be treated

- "Rejoice With It": Celebrate the successes or victories of other students regardless of the personal implications and consequences

Evangelism

When youth workers are committed to establishing and maintaining a narrative-missional model of youth ministry, students will be shepherded and shaped into students who are passionate about evangelism and will—

- Establish *intimate relationships* with others—they have a heart for other people and genuine friendships. Caring, listening, and loyalty characterize these friendships.

- Live a *Jesus-centered lifestyle*—in order for others to find the gospel relevant, believable, and accessible, we must live lives that reveal how the gospel continues to shape our own lives and communities.

- Tell a *compelling story*—the way students begin to share the gospel compels and interests people. A student realizes the gospel is active and looks to point people to God through various displays of God's restorative activity.

- Practice *time and patience*—students recognize the importance of walking the journey alongside people as they realize that most people won't receive the gospel the first time they hear it or see it proclaimed.

- Practice *acceptance and trust*—the realization of the need for time and patience also reveals to the student that many people for whom they proclaim the gospel will be skeptical, have different opinions and ideas about God, and perhaps even practice a preexisting belief system. Students become accepting of others, regardless of their religious affiliation.

Justice

When students begin to recognize the transformative nature of justice in their lives, they'll be able to consistently practice the following behaviors and practices:

- Becoming students of *pattern*—these are people who consistently serve others. A sporadic or even random restorative act here or there isn't enough. It helps, for sure, but it doesn't prove our desire to be people of service.

- Becoming students who *paint a picture* of who Jesus is by their actions, words, and decisions

- Becoming students who recognize the importance of being *present* with others—this isn't simply being around others. This is having the humility to put the needs of others first, giving them your complete and utter attention.

- Becoming students who are committed to living in *proximity* with others—to be "incarnate" is to be in the lives of people. We can't do that with an exclusive or reclusive mindset.

- Becoming *pillars* in the community—people who hold up others through their support, kindness, compassion, and so on.

- Becoming students who *pray* for their community and for the world

- Becoming students who know what it means to have a *posture* of humility

- Becoming students who rely on the *power* of God to fulfill God's mission in and through each one of us and around the world

Story-formed communities develop Story-formed students. Story-formed students live out the gospel, which is God's will, way, and work of providing salvation and justice through the gift of his Son, Jesus for all of humanity. The gospel lived out restores people to God.

As we've already discussed, in Luke 4 Jesus describes how he's come to bring the kingdom. In doing so, he'll bring the good news to the poor, prisoners, blind, and oppressed, or—as I described them in an earlier illustration—the least, lonely, lost, and left. The gospel articulated in both words and actions can restore the least, lonely, lost, and left to a new way of life.

For example, when the least are restored, they become the *blessed*. No longer without enough resources, the blessed, in turn, bless others and begin a life marked by spiritual growth and discovery, of discipleship. After restoration occurs, the lonely become those who now *belong*—to God and to people who are seeking to live as a community that invites others to share the faith experience together. The lost become found and, therefore, they can now *believe* in a rebirth and new life through the missional aspect of evangelism. Finally, those who are left alone as the exploited and demoralized of society are able to *become* something they've only dreamed of through the missional aspects of compassion and justice.[89]

The gospel restores people to God, self, others, and the surrounding world. And in doing so, it reveals and accomplishes the mission of God and the work of the church or our youth ministries.

People Group	Distinctive	Restored to	Restored Through
Poor	Least	Blessed	Discipleship
Prisoners	Lonely	Belong	Community
Blind	Lost	Believe	Evangelism
Oppressed	Left	Become	Justice

Story-formed students whose lives our caught up in a gospel of discipleship, community, evangelism, and justice and who represent a student community filled with authentic love and life can bring about salvation, healing, peace, and true restoration!

Reflection and Discussion Questions
Chapter 8—Application: God's Story as the Context for Our Behaviors and Expressions

• Of the four models of youth ministry suggested in chapter 8, which one does your youth ministry most closely resemble?

• In what ways are you helping the students in your youth ministry be and become storytellers?

• Chapter 8 suggests there are four primary areas of Christian formation—discipleship, community, evangelism, and justice. What do you like about this list? What would you suggest is missing from this list?

• On a scale of 1 to 10, with 10 being the highest, how close is your youth ministry to representing the components of community as outlined in 1 Corinthians 12:22-26?

• How would you describe a Jesus-centered lifestyle?

• What does it mean for your students to paint a picture of who Jesus is to the world around them?

CHAPTER 9

Implementation: Realizing a Narrative Approach to Youth Ministry

I've discovered three primary considerations when trying to implement a narrative approach to youth ministry. First, youth workers must have—at the very least—a conceptual knowledge of the *elements* of the spiritual journey. Second, youth workers must also have a basic understanding of transformative *environments*. Third, youth workers need a comprehensive understanding of their role as shepherds as they share in the *experiences* of their individual youth ministries.

While certainly not exhaustive—there's a lot more that youth workers need to be aware of as they guide, shape, and transform the lives of students—each of these considerations must be in place in order for any youth ministry to realize a narrative approach.

I simply offer them as suggestions to help you as you begin to lead change in your ministry, moving it from however it might be characterized now to however you wish it to be characterized in the future.[90] However, I believe these considerations are absolutely essential in the *implementation* of ministry programs and practices. It's my contention that without the knowledge and practice of these three considerations, a storytelling community cannot develop storytellers in the way of Jesus.

CONSIDERATION 1—THE ELEMENTS OF THE SPIRITUAL JOURNEY

We're all very different people. However, our lives share similar stories of spiritual growth and discovery. The particular situations and circumstances that comprise our stories may remain undeniably unique to us, but I've come to the conclusion that we all share a common journey, at least in form if not function. Nevertheless, the form or the mode in which we've encountered God, engaged in God's narrative and mission, and therefore entrusted God with our entire being is very analogous among us.

Over the years of studying Christian formation and the spiritual journey, I've come across a number of particularly helpful books written by great authors—from Fowler to Merton to Lawrence to de Sales to Matthewes-

Green to Tickle to Nouwen to Willard to Foster to Yancey to Peterson. And the list goes on and on. No one book, however, has had a greater influence on me than Janet Hagberg and Bob Guelich's *The Critical Journey: Stages in the Life of Faith* (Salem, Wis.: Sheffield Publishing Co., 2005).

Hagberg and Guelich offer a common, concise, and compelling look at the journey of faith and the stages that comprise the journey. To help you understand the elements of the spiritual journey, I'll adapt the ideas and concepts from *The Critical Journey* below.

In one of Brian McLaren's books, entitled *Finding Faith*, I came across another very simple way of viewing the stages of faith. Brian gives us four stages of faith that are memorable and uncomplicated: Simplicity, complexity, perplexity, and humility.

By mashing up the ideas and concepts of Hagberg and Guelich and McLaren, I hope to provide a straightforward yet in-depth understanding of the common spiritual journey that will make it easy to articulate it to others.

I don't believe any youth ministry can develop Story-formed students without the realization of Consideration 1.

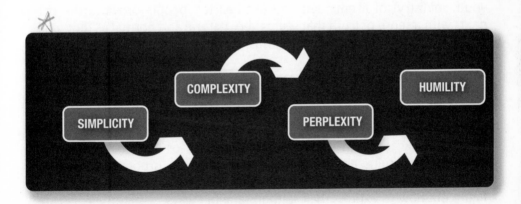

Simplicity

As you can see in the accompanying illustration, stage one of the spiritual journey is called *Simplicity*. At this stage in the life of a Christian, things are very uncomplicated. The reality is that there was an encounter with God, and at some point the new believer made the conscious decision to let God be the God of her life. The realization that a person cannot be her own god has come into play, and the decision has been made to let Jesus be King. Once independent of the things of God, a student has now decided to lean into God and God's narrative. Realizing the soul belongs to the kingdom of God, the student trusts Jesus as a real person.

Also at this stage of Simplicity, students become engaged in formation. They're growing and maturing in their identity with Jesus. They realize that a Christian is one who not only trusts Jesus as a person, but also begins to develop a set of beliefs and virtues through which to view all of life and to live by accordingly.

Since the mysterious choice to trust in Jesus has occurred, students view the things of God rather cleanly. They've trusted that there is a God and that Jesus is a real person who provides salvation for them. Therefore, to learn more about God and the way of Jesus seems natural and normal.

In addition, their experiences of being associated with a community (a youth ministry) of likeminded and like-hearted people provides the students with a sense of truth that seems very natural and normal as they walk with others who are walking with Jesus.

Another part of the Simplicity stage is the desire to serve, evangelize, and live justly. Students go beyond a decision to let God be God (which is obviously a decision, called repentance, that we make over and over again in our lives). They choose to go deeper in their discipleship or spiritual growth and discovery to begin reaching out. The ideas of God that were once intellectual pursuits, either personally collected or corporately gathered, become a practical reality. This movement into reality leads students to figure out how to express their faith in tangible ways.

During the stage of Simplicity, things make sense. Sure, there might be questions about the faith, a bit of confusion from time to time, and moments of slipping away from the things of God. But in general, students feel good about their faith. The journey of faith is understandable and tangible. It's simple. Of course, simple doesn't always mean easy. Nevertheless, faith is comprehendible and practicable, and that's what makes it simple.

Complexity

Somewhere along the way there is a situation or an event that takes the once-simple matters and makes them a bit more complicated. Something in the life of the student or the world around them moves their faith from within the stage of Simplicity into the stage of Complexity.

For me, it was the death of my grandfather when I was a teenager, the tragic world news of earthquakes, the falling of men and women serving in leadership roles around me, and a host of other matters that took my once-simple faith and made it complex.

For the students in your youth ministry, it might be world events, a new understanding of other religions, or it might be something more personal, such as their parents' divorce, a breakup with a boyfriend or girlfriend, not making the team, the disillusionment of friends, or any number of other matters that can make our faith complicated.

Of course, some of the situations, circumstances, or events that lead students into the stage of Complexity may seem inconsequential to us. Things like losing a game, not making the cheerleading team, not getting invited to the prom, and so on might be viewed by older people as being insignificant in the long run. However, they're huge matters of great significance to students, and for that reason we treat them as such.

Sure, the issues might get a little "bigger" as life rolls on (unemployment, bankruptcy, death of a spouse), but the issue isn't to compare our maturing lives with the maturing lives of our students. Naturally, we'll view the world from a different place in life, but it isn't the depth of the issues that moves our faith from being simple to complicated, it's about the shared mode of formation.

At the stage of Complexity, students become very introspective. They begin to question matters that were once accepted as truth. They begin to doubt God and the things of God when it seems like so much dissonance is happening around them. They begin to ask questions like, *Where is God? How could a loving God allow terrorists to kill hundreds of people? How could a God of grace and mercy be so uncompassionate and not feed the hungry people around the world or heal the sick? How could God allow my dad to beat my brother and me? Why is my sister a drug addict? Why am I addicted to porn? Why is my pastor having sex with someone other than his wife? Why do I have homosexual tendencies?*

The point is there are situations, circumstances, and events in the lives of students and in the world around them that cause their trust in Jesus to wane. The virtues they've been so diligently trying to live out also become somewhat dubious, and their faith becomes utterly complex.

Perplexity

After living in the realm of Complexity for a season of time, there occur yet more situations, circumstances, and events that push the students to a place of decision in their faith journeys and move students from the Complexity stage to Perplexity. Hagberg and Guelich call this place "the wall."

At this wall there is a new recognition that it's God versus me. Students have to decide to either walk away from faith, stop pursuing it so attentively and let it rest for a bit, or go deeper still, get over this wall, and let God be the God of their lives again.

At the wall, students come to grips with their immediate behaviors and expressions and make a conscious decision to either be the god of their own life, neglecting and forgetting the kingdom way, or to work through the perplexing matters—get over the wall, break through the wall, or dig a trench under the wall—to move their faith journey from the stage of Perplexity to Humility.

Humility

At the stage of humility, there's a renewed passion for the things of God. Emmanualism once again takes precedence, and they become more humble people as they love God and love others at deeper levels than they ever have before.

The intensity and the degree of frustration, pain, disbelief, and skepticism born out of the situations, circumstances, and events in the students' lives have been awful but at the same time good. Their experiences have led them through aspects of their faith journey to the place where they've begun a newer life—a life of humility or of placing God as the god of their lives.

This way of humility more deeply engages them in the narrative and mission of God and pushes them to revise their lives accordingly. The behaviors and expressions that were at one point so simple become clearer again, and there's a recommitment to the giving away of their lives. Humility reigns. The way of Jesus is again proclaimed and performed, and God becomes more than a collection of ideas and concepts. God becomes tangible both in how students encounter him and how others stumble upon him.

Traveling through this journey on a macro level and a micro level has an important outcome. You'll notice the illustration of the funnel (below). As the journey continues up the funnel, the plane at the top of the funnel expands. The longer the journey, the bigger the plane of humility, and that's the desired outcome of a life of Christian formation.

I believe it should go without saying, but it's important to note at this point that we can't manipulate the journey for our students, and they can't manipulate it for themselves. Remember our conversation about pilgrimage in chapter 2? We're on a pilgrimage to a special place. That special place is an expanding humility, and God is directing our travels.

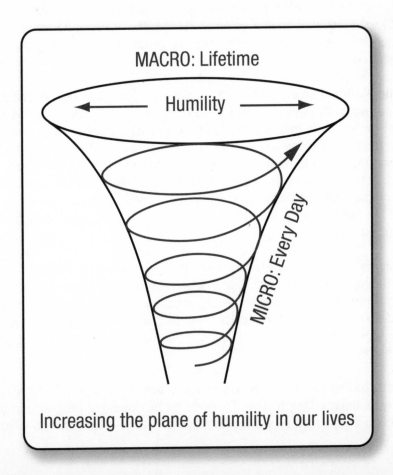

Increasing the plane of humility in our lives

Do you see yourself in the above description of a faith journey? Do you see how common the journey is? I hope you do. I hope these realizations allow you to possibly rethink the way you're doing youth ministry.

The fact of the matter is that we cannot expect our students to understand what the journey of faith is (or isn't) if we can't understand it and articulate it ourselves. A youth ministry cannot develop authentic Story-formed students who are passionately committed to God's narrative and mission if they're unaware of the spiritual journey.

CONSIDERATION 2—THE ATTRIBUTES OF TRANSFORMATIVE ENVIRONMENTS

Remember my description in chapter 5 of the youth worker as conservationist—one who cares for the ecosystem of youth ministry? We concluded (or at least I did) that an ecosystem in its most basic understanding has two components—environment (our ministry programs) and living organisms (our students).

We spent almost an entire chapter looking at the interaction between the environments we oversee and the students we shepherd. I offered you a model for applied theology made up of five aspects that help move theology from an intellectual pursuit to a practical reality for our students: Interaction, Intersection, Interchange, Identification, and Immersion. Each one is instrumental in the development of a theological foundation. And the foundation is the basis on which students will continue to build as they travel the faith journey, initiating and receiving more opportunity for spiritual growth and discovery.

Equally important to the development of the theological foundation is the students' environment. That's where students engage the narrative and mission of God at deeper levels. Healthy and effective environments that develop Story-formed students—and the youth workers that employ them—are keenly aware of three transformative elements: Time, space, and matter.

Without paying careful attention to these elements, a youth ministry can quickly be deemed ineffective. There might be dozens of programs in place; but if the programs are viewed and utilized as a means in and of themselves, then they aren't going to make the impact we all hope for, pray for, and expect.

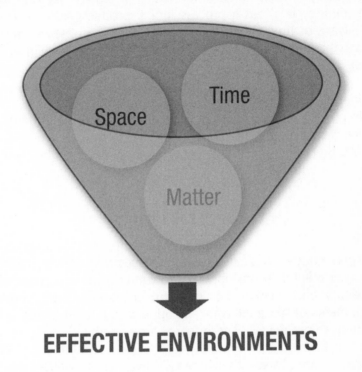

EFFECTIVE ENVIRONMENTS

Time

Humanity lives in two different kinds of time: *Chronos* and *kairos*. *Chronos* refers to time that we can divide, such as minutes, hours, years, and so on. *Kairos* refers to time in a qualitative sense, which is immeasurable time. *Kairos* time is characterized by what happens in it. When I speak of "time" as an element of transformative environments, I'm speaking of *kairos* that merges with *chronos* to inform our learning.[91]

Thus, when I talk about the time element of an effective environment, I'm not referring to the starting and ending times of your program (for example, 7 to 8:30 p.m. on a Sunday night). It isn't just about minutes and hours (*chronos*) but a pacing that cultivates a peace-filled, calm, and reflective atmosphere. What I mean is that whatever your program (environment) is, it should have a tempo that doesn't work to *impose* learning but instead *invites* learning.

An environment that's aware of time composes a sense of calm, stillness, and harmony that infuses all that it does. The environment isn't in a hurry to make Story-formed students. Rather, it remembers that transformational youth ministry is about a process, not a product. Also, an environment that's aware of time leaves room for students to observe and reflect on what's happening, what they're learning, and how they may practice it (*kairos*).

This doesn't mean you can't have an atmosphere of play—loud music, loud people playing games, or whatever fits your group of students. This simply means that during those party-like times, students are able to just be. Be calm. Be reflective. Be at peace. Be welcomed. Be who they are in the imago Dei—without something being imposed on them.

Space

Space isn't a buffer zone but a sacred, ascetically intriguing, and astonishing physical or mental "room" in which to contemplate and consider the wonder, beauty, and creativity of God's narrative and mission. In other words, environments of space cultivate the opportunity for students to encounter God in meaningful ways. These spaces are sacred.

By *sacred* I don't mean it's where God lives. God is all around us and in everything, of course. So sacred spaces aren't places to visit where God resides. Rather, sacred spaces are places where students can be more attentive to God's presence in their own lives. Sometimes these spaces are physical; sometimes they're more mental. Either way, space provides students with the opportunity to be fascinated and amazed by God and his presence in their lives.

On another note, the space you cultivate doesn't have to be about method as much as it is about mission. In other words, don't be faddish about using certain methods of programming for the sake of being hip or cool or in touch. On the contrary, be missional in your approach to creating spaces for students. Maybe that involves a dimly lit room with a wonderful ambiance, lighted candles, and beautiful art and icons. Or maybe space involves freedom from those things that distract our minds and hold us captive. At times I've felt free in the strangest places: My car, my mind, my office, my living room, a movie theatre, a coffee house, and so on.

Matter

Matter isn't the theme but the cooperating substance of an environment. Matter is the content that evokes the imagination, imparts for a recreated life, and inspires toward transformation. Matter is critical. There must be some material that transforms the lives of our students. There must be a basis for the program. It might be purely relational, it might be about leadership development, it might be about formation or any combination of the many issues we deal with in youth ministry. Whatever the reason for gathering, there must be content that helps our students imagine what a life with God could look like. The matter involved in our environments must be matter that motivates and stirs within our students a passion for the narrative and mission of God.

Typically, matter that accomplishes these purposes is experiential in nature and seeks to help students learn, not help teachers look or feel good. Matter that motivates and stirs the passions for God's narrative and mission is, of course, narrative-based. It's comprised of times of reflection, permission to ask questions, continuous dialogue, and situations in which to attempt to practice what's being learned.

Creating healthy and imaginative environments of time, space, and matter is vital to your youth ministry. Without these, programming will be insufficient and quickly become obsolete. As you seek to embrace these core aspects of transformative environments, be sure to connect all that you're doing to God's narrative and mission. For it's out of God's narrative and mission that we develop Story-formed students or storytellers who give witness to the work of the Holy Spirit.

Speaking of the Holy Spirit, be sure to remember his place and ministry in the world. Lean into that ministry (convicting, comforting, and so on), realizing and trusting that it's truly the Holy Spirit that works through youth workers, not vice versa.

CONSIDERATION 3—SHEPHERDING THROUGH SHARED EXPERIENCES

Youth workers are shepherds. We shepherd students through shared experiences and help them mature into missional people. To shepherd, in its simplest definition, is to tend, guide, care for, and protect. This is what we do—we shepherd our students. This isn't news to you, I'm sure. But what does it really mean to be a shepherd? Sometimes it's difficult to know what it looks like to tend, guide, care for, and protect the students in our ministry in practical ways.

Here is a great description of a shepherd:

> In early morning he led the flock from the fold, marching at its head to the spot where they were to be pastured. Here he watched them all day, taking care that none of the sheep strayed, and if any for a time eluded his watch and wandered away from the rest, seeking diligently till he found and brought it back. In those lands sheep require to be supplied regularly with water, and the shepherd for this purpose has to guide them either to some running stream or to wells dug in the wilderness and furnished with troughs. At night he brought the flock home to the fold, counting them as they passed under the rod at the door to assure himself that none were missing. Nor did his labors always end with sunset. Often he had to guard the fold through the dark hours from the attack of wild beasts, or the wily attempts of the prowling thief (see 1 Samuel 17:34).[92]

Keeping the above description of a shepherd in mind, what does it mean to be a shepherd? In other words, as a youth worker, what are the specific roles you play? Take a moment to grab a piece of paper and a pen (or go ahead and write in the margins of this book) and make a list of all the roles you play as a youth worker. We do a ton, eh? At times it's overwhelming.

One way to understand our role as shepherds is to put what we do into the categories of being an advocate, an advisor, and a guide. These are three roles we can play as we seek to infuse the students in our ministry with God's narrative and mission, and guide them toward becoming Story-formed students. These roles, of course, are only as good as the relationships we have with individual students. Also, I contend that youth workers shepherd their students best when the leaders see themselves as all three of these roles, not just one or another.

Advocate

An *advocate* can be defined as a person who stands in the gap, who roots for another person, who speaks in support of someone. We're taking the stance of a person who could be likened to a coach—someone who's an encourager, who gives opportunities, who helps students grow and develop and go deeper in their faith.

True advocating can occur only when there is a depth to the relationship. The greatest thing that youth ministry has going for it is the potential of healthy relationships. The hardest thing about youth ministry is cultivating healthy relationships. You can act as a good advocate only when you have relationships with students.

Healthy relationships consist of several key aspects, such as love, selflessness, care, listening, and so on. Regardless of how you might define a healthy relationship, it's a fact that without spending time with and sharing proximity to a person, you can't even begin to be a humble presence in someone's life. Transformational youth ministry is about genuine relationships with students.

Advisor

An *advisor* can be defined as a person who gives advice and guidance. We're taking the stance of a person who could be likened to a counselor or mentor for a student—someone who's there to give advice, assist in decision-making processes, and not just be an "answer giver" but a partner with the student in the practice of counseling.

True advising can occur only when there's discernment out of the depth of the shared experiences. What makes you a great shepherd is your ability to discern how to help students determine the next right thing to do in their lives. You can only be an effective co-discerner when you (1) are in tune to God's narrative and mission, (2) have a deep relationship with the particular student, and (3) discover how to discern appropriately based on the experiences of your own life and story.

Guide

A *guide* can be defined as a person who shows the way by directing, leading, and serving as a model. We're taking the stance of a person who could be likened to an adventure guide for students—someone who's walking the journey with them, pointing out things along the way, and allowing them to enjoy and encounter the learning that comes from the journey while giving directions when needed.

True guiding can happen only within the context of ongoing shared experiences that are built upon deep relationships and moments of helpful discernment.

The Advocate, Advisor, and Guide in Action

Role:	Advocate	Advisor	Guide
Action:	Ongoing unconditional support and place sharing	Ongoing counseling and crisis management	Ongoing encouragement and empowerment
Key Element:	Depth of shared experience	Discernment from experience	Direction toward future shared experience

If we wanted to take these three roles a bit further, it wouldn't be a stretch to see how they impact the shepherding of students through the journey of faith we examined earlier in this chapter. For example, an advocate might shepherd a student the most during the Simplicity stage of the faith journey. Functioning as an advisor might happen most often in the stages of Complexity and Perplexity. And finally, operating as a guide who models what it means to lean into the narrative of God and live out the mission of God might function best during the student's stage of Humility.

Advocate	Advisor	Guide
Simplicity	Complexity—Perplexity	Humility
Depth because you're NEAR to a student's life	Discernment in the NOW of a student's life	Direction for what's NEXT in the student's life

In summary, to develop Story-formed students who are engaged in the narrative and mission of God, carefully consider three things: The elements of the spiritual journey of faith, the environments in which you attempt to develop Story-formed students, and your role in shepherding students through shared experience.

Reflection and Discussion Questions
Chapter 9—Implementation: Realizing a Narrative Approach to Youth Ministry

- How do you "see yourself" in the funnel illustration on page 153?

- What are some of the circumstances that led you from the Simplicity stage to the Complexity stage?

- What are some of the circumstances that led you from the Complexity stage to the Perplexity stage?

- In what ways might students' doubts be a good thing?

- Chapter 9 suggests that there are three primary aspects to effective environments—time, space, and matter. What might be missing from this list?

- On a scale of 1 to 10, with 10 being the highest, how well are you doing with creating environments of time, space, and matter?

- Referring to the aspect of space, how does the word *sacred* strike you?

- Take a moment to make a list of all of the roles you play as a youth worker. (I'll get you on your way: Driver, chef, security, coach...)

- In your opinion, what does it mean to be an advocate?

- Regarding the key element of discernment, what experiences in your life allow for you to be a good counselor or someone who provides ongoing advice-giving and crisis management for students in your youth ministry?

- On a scale of 1 to 10, with 10 being the highest, how well are you functioning as a guide for your students? In what ways might you be more effective?

EPILOGUE

I want to conclude this book with four final thoughts. I hope and pray they will help you as you seek to implement the approach I've outlined in the previous chapters. Of course, because context is everything, you have the responsibility to take the ideas and concepts in this book and make them work for your cultural and ministry contexts. You're the expert! Only you (and your team) can decide the best way for you to enter into and engage the missio Dei. It's out of your heart and your specific calling that the missionary heart of God will be revealed and the mission of God (to restore the world to its intended wholeness) will be accomplished. Take seriously your role as a professional authority. Be a learner as you lead. Be a voice of hope. Be a person of character. Be a humble presence to all who interact with you. You, Youth Worker, are one of the *vital* and *valuable* agents that God is using to restore his world.

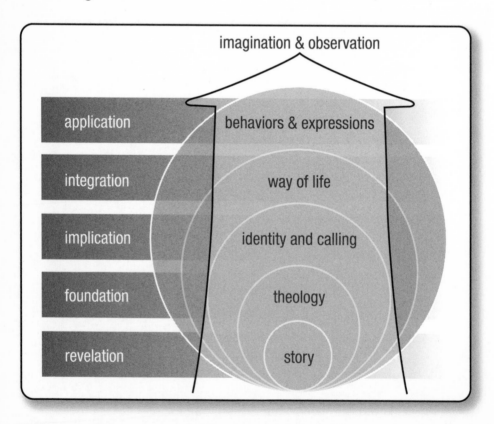

1. ENGAGE THE IMAGINATIONS OF STUDENTS AND BE A LIVING OBSERVATION

Sarah Arthur has written a terrific book entitled *The God-Hungry Imagination: The Art of Storytelling for a Postmodern Youth Ministry*. In her book Arthur uses a common definition of *imagination*. Arthur says, "Imagination is the image-making faculty that allows us to see and experience things that aren't immediately present to the senses."[93] She continues by providing five key areas of the function of the imagination—

1. Image-making: Seeing and experiencing things that are not immediately present.

2. Creativity: Demonstrating the mark or image of our creator.

3. "The mind's eye": The ability to discover and create relationships linking otherwise unconnected experiences, images, or ideas.

4. The organ of meaning: The organ of reason processes truth while the organ of imagination processes meaning.

5. The ability to say what something is like: The ability to think in analogies and metaphors.

Each of these is essential. However, in my opinion, no one is more important than the organ of meaning. If reason is the organ of truth, then imagination is the organ of meaning.[94]

As youth workers who are concerned with seeing our students engage in Christian formation, we must find creative ways to engage the imagination of our students as we teach truth. In doing so, we evoke both the organ of meaning and the organ of truth, and we can help our students engage the intelligible whole—the uniting of both truth and meaning.[95]

I believe this is one of the primary challenges we face in the Christian formation of our students. Too often we rely solely on the organ of reason to guide our students into Christian formation and either neglect or intentionally deny the use of the imagination. As we inspire, challenge, and equip our students with the necessary means to understand the Story of God, we must guide them not only in what is seen, but also in what is unseen.

For example, engaging the unseen through the imagination of students can—

- Give ways to contemplate new opportunities with God

- Provide for a new hope in faith or an alternate reality

- Provide new significances for old truths

- Position us in mysterious, variable patterns of life

- Change the way students view the world by helping them see how faith and life intersect

- Cultivate and grow new commitments to newfound spiritual discoveries

- Provide for a more robust prayer life as unseen matters are on equal footing with the seen matters of faith

- Provide fresh ways to interact with people and serve them

- Feed the soul with creative and artistic expressions of God connecting with a greater number of students and their distinctive affinities

- Connect the dots for students on what would otherwise be unassociated points of reality

The imagination is crucial to engaging students in Christian formation, which is obviously one of the major components of all of our communities of faith. Equally important is being a living observation. Our students need us to paint a picture of the way the world could be with the things of God in place. Students need to see youth workers as aspects of reason or as organs of truth. We don't have to be—nor can we be—perfect. But we must be actively engaged in living out what we teach. I know the Word of God is living and active, and I believe that with my whole being. However, the Word of God is most fully alive when it's activated through the lives of Christians.

In order for a narrative approach to youth ministry to work, the imagination of students must be engaged from the very beginning of the formation process. In order for the imagination to be most fully engaged, youth workers need to be a living observation—also from the beginning of the formation process. Remember this: You can't give away what you don't own!

2. THERE MUST BE AN INFORMED BALANCE IN THIS AND ANY APPROACH TO YOUTH MINISTRY

No one, including me, has the corner on the perfect model or approach to youth ministry. I know a lot of people who *think* they do. Some are just overly passionate people who believe in what they're teaching so much that they can't view any other way to do youth ministry. Other people are just that arrogant—they actually believe they've found God's way of doing youth ministry.

As you probably already know, there is no perfect model or approach to youth ministry. That's because culture is continuously changing; leadership is changing; methods are changing; and every few weeks a new pallet of books, tools, curricula, and so on arrives at your doorstep. There will always be people like me who come along and offer some new ideas for youth ministry. Be smart about your choices. Don't just trust the company logo on a book or the denominational headquarters that created the content. Instead, be selective and inform yourself as to the best and most effective resources or strategies of youth ministry.

Also realize the need for balance. And by *balance*, I mean the flexibility to roll with God's mysterious mission (as driven by the Holy Spirit) and the sensitivity to the Holy Spirit's movements to know when to get out of the way and when to remain constant. You're the one to bring balance to the accomplishment of God's mission through the three-part nature of the mission: The faith community, Scripture, and the cultural community. Balance, like many other areas of life, is a key to the effectiveness of any model of ministry.

3. THE DISCIPLINE AND PRACTICE OF SELF-TRANSCENDENCE IS KEY TO THE FORMATION OF YOU AND YOUR YOUTH MINISTRY

Self-transcendence resides in the conscience of the mind, the depths of the heart, and the cavern of the soul. It's the human ability to critique oneself.[96] Within every human being there exists within the mind, heart, and soul an internal dialogue. This dialogue is proof of the morality of God. Having been created in the image of God, humans have an internal moral standard that works to second-guess the words, actions, and thoughts of humanity. It's continually helping to resolve the inner confusion and conflict of the mind, heart, and soul, pushing a person away from what's wrong and broken and pulling her toward what is right and whole.

One of the best things we can do as human beings is practice the discipline of self-transcendence. That is, to step outside of ourselves—if even for a moment—to become an onlooker and critique what we see. This practice helps us realize who we are and who we're becoming. I suppose in a very practical way the practice of self-transcendence is similar to that of a golfer who videotapes her swing to find weak points, or the dancer who watches himself on video to find ways to improve his form, or a storyteller who listens to a recording of himself telling a story in order to determine ways to be a better storyteller. Self-transcendence isn't about comparing your life to anyone else's—except Christ's. It's about assessing your individual spiritual life.

Obviously, the practice of the discipline of self-transcendence requires solitude, personal reflection, honesty, sacrifice, openness, determination, and ultimately transformation. It's a difficult process—even brutal at times, as quite often we're harder on ourselves than we are on anyone else. However, it's a process that produces the true self, rather than negating the self.

Self-transcendence is authentic self-realization.[97] However, it isn't the end of human development, as humanistic theories of development might assume and endorse. Instead, in many ways it's the beginning of lasting spiritual formation, as we're called to deny our selves and give our lives away to the work of God.

Self-transcendence leads us toward a few things: Other-centeredness, hospitality, and reconciliation.[98] These three aspects are critical for your personal commitment, as well as your corporate commitment to the missio Dei. The ability to guide students into Christian formation is directly dependent on our ability to give of ourselves and be generous with our time, talents, and treasures. It involves putting others (namely students) first in our lives and allowing that generosity to lead students toward a new wholeness with God, self, others, and the world.

4. YOU ARE A PILGRIM

Trust the way, for trust is a key to your students' transformation through the missio Dei. To trust is hard. Of course, that's what faith is all about—trusting God. However, far too often our insecurities, fears, personal desires, and other obstacles keep us from a life marked by trust.

I believe Brennan Manning wrote one of the most influential books on the topic of trust—*Ruthless Trust: The Ragamuffin's Path to God*. Manning's work will take you to places in your soul where you've likely never gone before. But once you've visited them, they are places that you'll be certain to no longer hold as rare. Ruthless trust can ultimately be summarized as this: "Faith in the person of Jesus and hope in his promise."[99]

If we're going to be youth workers who see transformational youth ministry impact the lives of our students, we must become people of trust. We need to become people who allow trust to give definition to our lives, impact the decisions we make, and shape the words we choose and the actions we live out. We need trust to change the way we view our relationships with God, self, others, and the surrounding world. We need to be people who move beyond trust as an abstract thought and move into a realm of trust that's authentic, tangible, and experienced.[100]

According to Manning, trust is "a movement into obscurity, into the undefined, into ambiguity, not into some predetermined, clearly delineated plan for the future."[101] Trust is imperative to the pilgrim who leaves what is undoubtedly certain, safe, and confident and travels into the way of the unknown without "any rational explanation to justify the decision or guarantee the future."[102]

The world of youth ministry needs youth workers who:

- Trust the Mission of God—it can be difficult to resist the urge to fabricate situations and events that are missional, rather than find where God is already at work and join in his activity there. We have to resist the urge to forge or construct something from nothing and let God be God, trusting that his mission is as active as our desire to fabricate. This doesn't mean we aren't leaders or that we don't take advantage of a situation that allows us to bring about the goals of God's mission—salvation and justice. It simply means we're people who are working out God's dream for the world, rather than looking for ways to make our dream noticeable, impressive, and enchanting. We're on this planet to make God famous, not to create a legacy of our own efforts.

- Trust in the Journey—Each of us is on a journey. We're in the process of continual spiritual discovery and growth. The journey, like the mission of God, isn't ours to plot. Rather, the spiritual journey is one of wandering or sojourn or even still peregrination—the act of allowing God to take a person where God wants that person to go. Youth workers are driven people. We're often so driven, however, that we can't think of any other way but our own. It isn't always done in arrogance. Sometimes it's just the sheer desire for something that causes us to do whatever it takes to obtain it. This trait isn't always a negative thing. But when it involves pushing our own way or trying to pave our own path, it can have negative implications. A trusting person is on a pilgrimage to wherever and cares more about the journey—and the One who directs her next steps—than the destination.

- Trust in the People They're Becoming—The journey makes us into who we are and who we're becoming. The journey, because it's one of wandering and not wanting, produces within us a trust that transcends the fears we own but work so hard to get rid of. We've been given what we need in our core competencies, gifts, unique skills, and so on to carry out the specific calling God has for our lives. We trust that the wandering isn't in vain, but rather in victory—a victory over the very fears that can often control us and cause us to want to fabricate. In this trust we must realize that God has given us exactly what we need to carry out his mission. I don't believe God places in our hearts an authentic calling to a specific role in his mission and then leaves us ill equipped to carry it out. Notwithstanding the things that make us trust in God more, such as various trials or tragedies, our journey is making available to us the opportunity to become exactly what God wants us to become. Trust the journey and lean into it knowing that God shapes us in his way, not in our own way. The various situations in which God places us and the circumstances and events of those situations that he allows us to endure are all part of living out of a trusted journey.

- Trust the People Around Them—If we believe God has us on an intentional journey of spiritual discovery and growth, then we must believe God has others on similar journeys. The people around you won't have the same core competencies, gifts, and skills as you do. That's what makes teams work. Don't expect that everyone will be like you, sharing in your specific calling and with the same amount of passion. Others will have their own specific calling and passions. It's when youth workers recognize and value this reality that true collaboration can breed authentic transformation. Trusting the people around you is another way of trusting God—just as you'd trust God with your own journey.

- Trust Their Intuition—The collection of experiences that God has led you into and through, coupled with your personal composition and the experiences of those around you, contributes to your instinctive knowledge. Your instinctive knowledge isn't to be taken lightly—it's part of who you are. I suppose when it's defined simply as "a hunch, a guess, or a whim," intuition might be considered nothing more than speculation. However, actual intuition that's born out of who you are and who you're becoming, in my opinion, is just as important an aspect of leadership as vision, strategy, and execution. Often it's our intuition that leads us to a vision, strategy, and execution plan in the first place. The insights and feelings we have are important. Don't suppress them as though modernity was right in saying that reason and fact are more important than feeling. Feeling is from God, and it's what often leads us to use our imaginations and toward inspiration. Trust your intuitions, for they're the very things that may direct you and your ministry to realizing maximum impact in the lives of your students.

TRUSTING IN THE WILL, WAY, AND WORK OF GOD

Trust produces a non-anxious presence. It provides for an atmosphere of calm, peace, joy, and harmony with God, self, others, and the surrounding world. Being a person of trust enables youth workers to combat the hurried pace, changing culture, and constant uncertainties of working with youth with courage, compassion, confidence, and conviction. Trust is the assurance that even in the midst of all that might arise in life and ministry, the will, way, and work of God in Christ Jesus and through the church won't fail. Do you trust the missionary heart of God to restore the world to its intended wholeness? Do you trust the mission of God to rearrange your life and ministry accordingly?

Isaiah 52:7-10

How beautiful on the mountains

are the feet of those who bring good news,

who proclaim peace,

who bring good tidings,

who proclaim salvation,

who say to Zion,

"Your God reigns!"

Listen! Your watchmen lift up their voices;

together they shout for joy.

When the LORD returns to Zion,

they will see it with their own eyes.

Burst into songs of joy together,

you ruins of Jerusalem,

for the LORD has comforted his people,

he has redeemed Jerusalem.

The LORD will lay bare his holy arm

in the sight of all the nations,

and all the ends of the earth will see

the salvation of our God.

APPENDIX A

One way to discover, understand, and interpret the cultural distinctiveness of the students in our communities is to take a look at their intellectual, physical and emotional, spiritual, and social characteristics. Use the following questions to help you better navigate the fluidity of the cultural context of your youth ministry.[103]

INTELLECTUAL

• How are students choosing to learn and discover new information?

• How have the ways students learn changed in the past 10 or 15 years?

• How does your community value knowledge and education?

• What do students in your community do after graduation?

PHYSICAL AND EMOTIONAL

• What characterizes the appearance of your male students?

• What characterizes the appearance of your female students?

• What shapes the self-image of your students the most?

• What are the most stressful situations your students are facing?

SPIRITUAL

- What factors are influencing the spiritual development of your students the most?

- What spiritual questions are your students asking?

- In what areas of spiritual matters do your students doubt?

- In what areas have you seen your students growing spiritually?

SOCIAL

- What social groups do you notice among the students in your communities?

- What are the main issues, needs, or factors in your communities that are influencing students?

- How are the students in your community affected by social pressures?

- What activities (sports or otherwise) are your students most involved in?

- In what ways are you seeing a rise in student volunteerism?

APPENDIX B

Take the next few minutes to do the exercises below. They will help guide your thoughts and prayers. This is an opportunity for you to express your love and commitment to God.

REPENT

Recognize...

Ask God to reveal areas in which you've sinned and gone against his ways.

"Search me, God, and know my heart; test me and know my anxious thoughts." (Psalm 139:23)

Confess...

Quietly share the specifics of your struggle with God.

"Those who conceal their sins do not prosper, but those who confess and renounce them find mercy." (Proverbs 28:13)

Release...

Open your hands and give your sins to God. Try to feel the reality that God will lift this burden from you.

"If we confess our sins, he is faithful and just and will forgive us our sins and purify us from all unrighteousness." (1 John 1:9)

Receive...

Embrace the truth that God has forgiven you and will give you strength to follow him and resist temptation.

"No temptation has overtaken you except what is common to us all. And God is faithful; he will not let you be tempted beyond what you can bear. But when you are tempted, he will also provide a way out so that you can endure it." (1 Corinthians 10:13)

BELIEVE

Spend a minute meditating on these verses and write a prayer response.

"As the Father has loved me, so have I loved you. Now remain in my love. If you keep my commands, you will remain in my love, just as I have kept my Father's commands and remain in his love. I have told you this so that my joy may be in you and that your joy may be complete." (John 15:9-11)

FOLLOW

Following Jesus is an active pursuit of becoming like him. It's letting his Spirit shape us and form us into his image.

"Yet you, LORD, are our Father. We are the clay, you are the potter; we are all the work of your hand." (Isaiah 64:8)

"But the fruit of the Spirit is love, joy, peace, patience, kindness, goodness, faithfulness, gentleness and self-control...Since we live by the Spirit, let us keep in step with the Spirit." (Galatians 5:22-23, 25)

Take a moment and ask God's Spirit to cultivate his fruit in your life. Ask for specific help and growth in areas where you struggle to exhibit the fruit of the Spirit.

ENDNOTES

1. I first learned of the word *glocal* a few years ago. It was in the book *A Is for Abductive: The Language of the Emerging Church* by Leonard Sweet, Brian McLaren, and Jerry Haselmayer (Zondervan, 2003). The term is thrown around in a variety of circles; therefore, it's collected its fair share of variable definitions. Simply put, the word *glocal*, as I use it here, refers to individuals or communities who have a passion to think globally and act locally.

2. Take a minute to check out http://youthnoise.com/mci/. When you look into the hearts and souls of literally thousands of teenagers who desire to use their cause to change the world, it's sure to refresh your heart and energize your soul.

3. Esther Dodgen, *Flowers Along the Path: Collected Wisdom for Your Spiritual Journey* (Uhrichsville, Ohio: Barbour Publishing, 2001), 352.

4. Arthur A. Rouner Jr., *Someone's Praying, Lord: A Book of Prayers* (Englewood Cliffs, NJ: Prentice-Hall Inc., 1970), 199.

5. Frederick Buechner, *The Hungering Dark* (New York: HarperOne, 1985), 33.

6. Walter Rauschenbusch, *For God and the People: Prayers of the Social Awakening* (Chicago: The Pilgrim Press, 1909), 83–84.

7. Michael now trains youth workers in the art of chronological Bible storying through his company Echo the Story (echothestory.com). Matt still works with me at Youthfront, providing oversight to all of our youth worker initiatives. Doug has a job in the "real" world, volunteers at his church, works with us a bit at Youthfront, and blogs at the highly acclaimed perigrinatio.com. Seth is presently the pastor of students at Woodland Hills Church in St. Paul, Minnesota.

8. See pages 94–100 of Michael Novelli's book *Shaped by the Story: Helping Students Encounter God in a New Way* (Zondervan/Youth Specialties, 2008).

9. Scot McKnight, *The Jesus Creed: Loving God, Loving Others* (Brewster, Mass.: Paraclete Press, 2004). Scot offers a brilliant way to view the life and ministry of Jesus though the lens of the Great Commandments. I highly recommend this book as a starting point for understanding Christian formation.

10. Gabriel Fackre, *The Christian Story: A Narrative Interpretation of Basic Christian Doctrine* (Grand Rapids, Mich.: Eerdmans, 1996), 27.

11. Charles Van Engen, *Mission on the Way: Issues in Mission Theology* (Grand Rapids, Mich.: Baker Academic, 1996), 54.

12. Van Engen, *Mission on the Way*, 55.

13. Van Engen, *Mission on the Way*, 52.

14. There are many, many systematic theologians who understand and even function with the organization of their ideas of God out of the metanarrative. I don't mean to slam the systematic theologian—or systematic theology, for that matter. However, my experience is that most youth workers aren't theologians. Therefore, I submit that most youth workers who've been taught systematic theology have a hard time organizing ideas of God out of the narrative juxtaposed to the category.

15. Lesslie Newbigin, *The Open Secret: An Introduction to the Theology of Mission* (Grand Rapids, Mich.: Eerdmans, 1995), 95.

16. Richard Bauckham, *Bible and Mission: Christian Witness in a Postmodern World* (Grand Rapids, Mich.: Baker Academic, 2004), 88.

17. Bauckham, *Bible and Mission*, 88.

18. Bauckham, *Bible and Mission*, 92.

19. Bauckham, *Bible and Mission*, 93.

20. Newbigin, *The Open Secret*, 95.

21. Bauckham, *Bible and Mission*, 98.

22. Van Engen, *Mission on the Way*, 49.

23. David J. Bosch, *Transforming Mission: Paradigm Shifts in the Theology of Mission* (Maryknoll, N.Y.: Orbis Books, 1991), 390.

24. Bosch, *Transforming Mission*, 390.

25. Christopher J. H. Wright, *The Mission of God: Unlocking the Bible's Grand Narrative* (Downers Grove, Ill.: InterVarsity Press Academic, 2006), 23.

26. Bosch, *Transforming Mission*, 10.

27. It's important to remember the Christological significance of the mission of God. Sometimes when referring to the mission of God and its origination in the heart of God, the focus can be solely placed on God as Father and therefore neglect God as Son. The mission of God is as much about Jesus and his person and work as it is about God. For more on the person and work of Jesus, refer to chapter 6 in this book.

28. Bosch, *Transforming Mission*, 392.

29. Van Engen, *Mission on the Way*, 26–27.

30. Van Engen, *Mission on the Way*, 27.

31. Obviously, it's important to remember that we ourselves don't do the "freeing." God frees our students from the things that hold them captive. We're simply conduits of God's grace, mercy, love, and protection. Liberation happens when students meet *God*, not merely the people of God. True, the people of God—the church—can be a liberating body. However, real liberation only happens through the gospel.

32. Millard J. Erikson, *Christian Theology* (Grand Rapids, Mich.: Baker Academic, 1998), 901.

33. See my article "The Disciple as an Illustration of Truth" (*Re-imaging Youth Ministry*, March/April 2007) for more on what it looks like to live as an illustration of truth. (http://www.anewkindofyouthministry.com/wp-content/uploads/2008/01/rym-marchapril-07.pdf)

34. This is Jeremy Del Rio's definition of justice, which was shared in Chap Clark and Kara Powell's *Deep Justice in a Broken World: Helping Your Kids Serve Others and Right the Wrongs Around Them* (Grand Rapids, Mich.: Zondervan/Youth Specialties, 2007), 10.

35. Office for Social Justice St. Paul and Minneapolis, "Major Themes from Catholic Social Teaching," http://www.osjspm.org/major_themes.aspx (accessed 4/25/09).

36. Brennan Manning, *A Glimpse of Jesus: The Stranger to Self-Hatred* (New York: Harper Collins, 2003), 29.

37. Doug Lipman, *Improving Your Storytelling: Beyond the Basics for All Who Tell Stories in Work or Play* (Atlanta: August House Publishers, 1999), 17.

38. Mark Miller, *Experiential Storytelling: (Re)Discovering Narrative to Communicate God's Message* (Grand Rapids, Mich: Zondervan/Youth Specialties, 2003), 33. This book, in my opinion, started a wave of thinking and practice in "story" for anyone doing ministry in a postmodern construct, especially those of us in youth ministry. For me personally, Mark's book was instrumental in helping me shift my thinking and practices as I struggled so desperately to minister to changing students in a changing culture.

39. Daniel Taylor, *Tell Me a Story: The Life-Shaping Power of Our Stories* (St. Paul, Minn.: Bog Walk Press, 2001), 21.

40. Taylor, *Tell Me a Story*, 21.

41. Henri J. M. Nouwen, *Sabbatical Journey: The Diary of His Final Year* (New York: The Crossroad Publishing Company, 1998), 10.

42. Bosch, *Transforming Mission*, 390. (The bracketed text is my addition to Bosch's statement.)

43 Marty Neumeier, ed., *The Dictionary of Brand* (Vancouver, B.C.: AIGA Center for Brand Experience, 2004), 30.

44. Neumeier, *The Dictionary of Brand*, 29.

45. I owe this point to Eric Venable. I heard him say this phrase in response to a question he was asked at a seminar he was leading called *Questioning Youth Ministry? Helping Students Build Faith Counter-intuitively*, November 21, 2008, Nashville, National Youth Workers Convention by Youth Specialties.

46. I wrote a chapter called "Reculturing Education: From Teacher-Centered Curricula to Learner-Centered Environments" in my first book, *A New Kind of Youth Ministry* (Zondervan/Youth Specialties, 2006), that can help you. It offers a brief summary of what it means to help students work *through* the information, as opposed to giving them more information.

47. Bosch, *Transforming Mission*, 390.

48. Bosch, *Transforming Mission*, 389-390.

49. Newbigin, *The Open Secret*, 59.

50. Newbigin, *The Open Secret*, 57.

51. Newbigin, *The Open Secret*, 56.

52. Newbigin, *The Open Secret*, 59.

53. Bosch, *Transforming Mission*, 390.

54. First Peter 2:9 says, "But you are a chosen people, a royal priesthood, a holy nation, God's special possession, that you may declare the praises of him who called you out of darkness into his wonderful light."

55. Roundtable, "Transformers: Ministry That Changes Lives," *Network Magazine* (Fall 2007), 6, http://www.youthworkers.net/index.cfm/fuseaction/net-mag.viewarticle/NetMagID/24/ArticleID/167 (accessed 4/25/09).

56. This idea is really a mash-up of ideas from David Kolb and Charles Van Engen. Kolb is an expert in experiential learning. His book *Experiential Learning: Experience as the Source of Learning Development* (Prentice Hall, 1983) is highly acclaimed and a staple in nearly every educator's library. And I've already used some of Van Engen's thinking from his book *Mission on the Way* in this book. Van Engen gives a great illustration of contextualizing the Scriptures into various community contexts. Therefore, I owe this point to both Kolb and Van Engen.

57. Terry Doyle, *Helping Students Learn in a Learner-Centered Environment* (Sterling, Va.: Stylus Publishing, 2008), 44.

58. Doyle, *Helping Students Learn in a Learner-Centered Environment*, 45.

59. Doyle, *Helping Students Learn in a Learner-Centered Environment*, 45.

60. Patty Griffin, "When It Don't Come Easy," *Impossible Dream* (Ato Records, 2004).

61. David Elkind, *All Grown Up and No Place to Go: Teenagers in Crisis* (Cambridge, Mass.: Da Capo Press, 1998), 18.

62. Elkind, *All Grown Up and No Place to Go*, 19.

63. L. L. Thurstone, "The Vectors of the Mind," (*Psychological Review* 41, 1-32, 1934).

64. http://en.wikipedia.org/wiki/Big_Five_personality_traits (accessed 4/25/09).

65. Dennis F. Kinlaw, *Let's Start With Jesus: A New Way of Doing Theology* (Grand Rapids, Mich.: Zondervan, 2005), 101.

66. Scot McKnight, *The Jesus Creed: Loving God, Loving Others* (Brewster, Mass: Paraclete Press, 2004).

67. Joel B. Green, Scot McKnight, I. Howard Marshall, *Dictionary of Jesus and the Gospels* (Downers Grove, Ill.: InterVarsity Press, 1992).

68. Hebrews 2:17 says, "For this reason he had to be made like his brothers and sisters in every way, in order that he might become a merciful and faithful high priest in service to God, and that he might make atonement for the sins of the people."

69. Hebrews 4:15 says, "For we do not have a high priest who is unable to empathize with our weaknesses, but we have one who has been tempted in every way, just as we are—yet he did not sin."

70. Matthew 28:18 says, "Then Jesus came to them and said, 'All authority in heaven and on earth has been given to me.'"

71. John 18:36-37 says, "Jesus said, 'My kingdom is not of this world. If it were, my servants would fight to prevent my arrest by the Jewish leaders. But now my kingdom is from another place.' 'You are a king, then!' said Pilate. Jesus answered, 'You say that I am a king. In fact, the reason I was born and came into the world is to testify to the truth. Everyone on the side of truth listens to me.'"

72. Isaiah 61:1-2 says, "The Spirit of the Sovereign LORD is on me, because the LORD has anointed me to proclaim good news to the poor. He has sent me to bind up the brokenhearted, to proclaim freedom for the captives and release from darkness for the prisoners, to proclaim the year of the LORD's favor and the day of vengeance of our God, to comfort all who mourn."

73. There is so much more in Luke 4:14-21 to study. I'd encourage you and your team to spend some time reading and reflecting on this passage so you might uncover some of the contextual aspects of Jesus' rejection, Rome's rule, the hearing of the reading by the people of Israel, and so on.

74. For more on this, seek the wisdom of Scot McKnight in his work *Embracing Grace: A Gospel for All of Us* (Brewster, Mass.: Paraclete Press, 2005).

75. I realize it's dangerous to reduce the gospel down to four chapters. However, I also realize it's dangerous not to give our students a way in which they might articulate the gospel. I confess there's a serious tension inside of me as I want so desperately to avoid the modern means of what might appear to be a reductionist's view of the gospel yet assist our postmodern students with a means that helps them share God's Story with their families, friends, coworkers, teammates, and others.

76. Stan Grenz was a friend to many of us. His writing and lecturing was very helpful in the formation of my thinking on postmodern ministry to youth and young adults. Stan died in March 2005 after suffering a brain hemorrhage. I still dig up my notes from his lectures and go back and read all of the highlighted areas of his books in my personal collection. If you're unfamiliar with Stan or his works, then at the very least you should make an effort to Google him.

77. Stanley J. Grenz, *A Primer on Postmodernism* (Grand Rapids, Mich.: Eerdmans, 1996), 167-174.

78. Grenz, *A Primer on Postmodernism*, 167.

79. Grenz, *A Primer on Postmodernism*, 169.

80. Grenz, *A Primer on Postmodernism*, 171.

81. Grenz, *A Primer on Postmodernism*, 172.

82. Ephesians 1:22-23 says, "And God placed all things under his feet and appointed him to be head over everything for the church, which is his body, the fullness of him who fills everything in every way."

83. Some of the content in this chapter comes directly from a training experience that Sonlife (now Youthfront) developed when I was president. I'm indebted to Matt Wilks, Doug Jones, Michael Novelli, Jamie Roach, Nathan Vawser, and Seth McCoy for how that training experience and this chapter have shaped up over the last couple of years. Their creative and editorial contributions have been tremendously helpful.

84. Scot McKnight, *The Jesus Creed: Loving God, Loving Others* (Brewster, Mass.: Paraclete Press, 2004), 72.

85. Donald P. McNeill, Henri J. M. Nouwen, and Douglas A. Morrison, *Compassion: A Reflection on the Christian Life* (New York: Doubleday, 1982), 21.

86. I'm not sure where I first heard this word *Emmanualism*. I didn't think it up, but I love it! I do know that Frank Mercadante, a friend and the executive director of Cultivation Ministries, and I talked about this word on occasion.

87. Eugene Peterson, *The Jesus Way: A Conversation on the Ways That Jesus Is the Way* (Grand Rapids, Mich.: Eerdmans, 2007), 7.

88. Peterson, *The Jesus Way*, 7.

89. I owe this point to Doug Jones, a longtime friend and ministry partner. We were driving from Kansas City to Minneapolis to do some training, and this conversation came up in the car.

90. John Kotter wrote a book called *Leading Change* (Cambridge, Mass.: Harvard Business School Press, 1996). If you're thinking you may have the privilege of leading change in your ministry, then you need to find this book. Kotter outlines an eight-step process for leading change that I've used on several occasions. I've found Kotter's work extremely helpful in my leadership experiences.

91. Frederick Buechner, *The Hungering Dark* (New York: HarperOne, 1985), 104.

92. Matthew G. Easton, definition of *shepherd* found on the "Dictionaries" page of BibleGateway.com, and in the online Bible Encyclopedia of

ChristianAnswers.net, http://www.christiananswers.net/dictionary/shepherd.html (accessed 4/25/09).

93. Sarah Arthur, *The God-Hungry Imagination: The Art of Storytelling for Postmodern Youth Ministry* (Nashville: Upper Room, 2007), 42.

94. Arthur, *The God-Hungry Imagination*, 49.

95. Arthur, *The God-Hungry Imagination*, 50.

96. Dennis F. Kinlaw, *Let's Start With Jesus: A New Way of Doing Theology* (Grand Rapids, Mich.: Zondervan, 2005), 95.

97. Les L. Steele, *On the Way: A Practical Theology of Christian Formation* (Grand Rapids, Mich.: Baker Book House, 1990), 112.

98. Steele, *On the Way*, 112.

99. Brennan Manning, *Ruthless Trust: The Ragamuffin's Path to God* (San Francisco: Harper Collins, 2002), 178.

100. Manning, *Ruthless Trust*, 165.

101. Manning, *Ruthless Trust*, 12.

102. Manning, *Ruthless Trust*, 13.

103. Material taken from *Enroute: Exploring Transformational Youth Ministry*, a one-day training event for youth workers held in various cities around North America. For more information on Enroute, visit www.barefootministries. com. Enroute: Exploring Transformational Youth Ministry by Chris Folmsbee, Copyright Youthfront, Inc., ©2006-2009. All rights reserved.

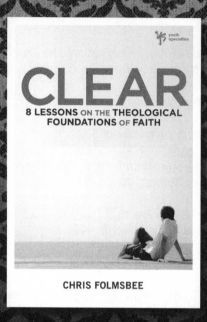

CLEAR

8 LESSONS ON THE THEOLOGICAL FOUNDATIONS OF FAITH

CHRIS FOLMSBEE

For teens whose faith seems a little blurry, *Clear* will help put it into focus. The interactive exercises in this book will help students develop a better understanding of God and his truths so they can be more like Jesus. As they study God, Jesus, the Holy Spirit, Humanity, Sin, Salvation, the Church, and Heaven, they'll begin to see their faith more clearly.

Clear
8 Lessons on the Theological Foundations of Faith
Chris Folmsbee

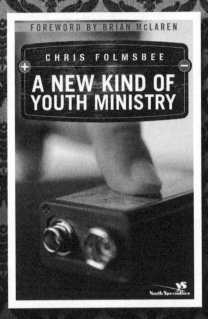

FOREWORD BY BRIAN McLAREN

CHRIS FOLMSBEE

A NEW KIND OF YOUTH MINISTRY

A New Kind of Youth Ministry challenges you to take a fresh look at your mnistry through the concept of "reculturing"—the act of changing the way things are done or simply creating a culture of change. No fly-bynight, change-for-the-sake-of-change concept, it's about altering our paradigms for the sake of life change. You'll find that as you step back and look at your ministry through a new lens, the possibilities on the horizon are limitless.

A New Kind of Youth Ministry

Chris Folmsbee

youth
specialties

youth specialties

ALL ABOUT YOUTH MINISTRY

RESOURCES FOR YOUR MINISTRY, YOUR STUDENTS, AND YOUR SOUL

THE YOUTH MINISTRY SURVIVAL GUIDE Kageler

HEAR AND DO Shafer

IMAGINATIVE PRAYER FOR YOUTH MINISTRY OESTREICHER & WARNER

BETTER SAFE THAN SUED CRABTREE

SHAPED BY THE STORY NOVELLI

LOSE YOUR COOL HUNTER

MSSS :: MY FAITH JOHNSTON & OESTREICHER

it's not easy being green sleeth

RELATIONSHIPS UNFILTERED ROOT

LEAVE A FOOTPRINT BAKER

TEENAGE GIRLS Olson ZONDERVAN

STUDIES ON THE GO · ROMANS polich

MIDDLE SCHOOL MINISTRY Oestreicher & Rubin

HOW TO VOLUNTEER LIKE A PRO HANCOCK

HELP! I'M A SMALL GROUP LEADER! TRAINING VIDEO

GOOD SEX 2.0 HANCOCK & PO

YOUTH MINISTRY 3.0 OESTREICHER

EVANGELISM REMIXED RAHN & LINHART

ESSENTIAL LEADERSHIP LEADER'S GUIDE POWELL

DOWNTIME YACONELLI

CONNECT MCKEE

CREATIVE BIBLE LESSONS IN ROMANS CLARK

AWAKEN YOUR CREATIVITY CHRISTIE

A TALE OF TWO YOUTH WORKERS VENABLE

YOU TEACH VOL 4 THE SKIT GUYS

YOUTH CULTURE 101 Mueller

THE SPACE BETWEEN MUELLER

The complete NEW TESTAMENT resource for YOUTH WORKERS volume 1

UNLEASHING GOD'S WORD Shafer

WHAT DO I DO WHEN TEENAGERS ARE VICTIMS OF ABUSE?

WHEN CHURCH KIDS GO BAD CHRISTIE

BOOKS FOR TEENS

MIDDLE SCHOOL RESOURCES

CURRICULUM

YOUTH WORKER DEVELOPMENT

PROGRAMMING

Share Your Thoughts

With the Author: Your comments will be forwarded to the author when you send them to *zauthor@zondervan.com*.

With Zondervan: Submit your review of this book by writing to *zreview@zondervan.com*.

Free Online Resources at
www.zondervan.com

Zondervan AuthorTracker: Be notified whenever your favorite authors publish new books, go on tour, or post an update about what's happening in their lives at www.zondervan.com/authortracker.

Daily Bible Verses and Devotions: Enrich your life with daily Bible verses or devotions that help you start every morning focused on God. Visit www.zondervan.com/newsletters.

Free Email Publications: Sign up for newsletters on Christian living, academic resources, church ministry, fiction, children's resources, and more. Visit www.zondervan.com/newsletters.

Zondervan Bible Search: Find and compare Bible passages in a variety of translations at www.zondervanbiblesearch.com.

Other Benefits: Register yourself to receive online benefits like coupons and special offers, or to participate in research.

ZONDERVAN®

ZONDERVAN.com/
AUTHORTRACKER
follow your favorite authors